唐代五绝品读与英译研究系列

教育部人文社会科学研究一般项目"唐代五绝及其韵体英译研究"
(项目编号:14YJA740039)资助出版

唐代五绝101首及其韵体英译并注

101 Tang Dynasty's Quatrains with Five Chinese Characters to Each Line, Their Translations into English Verse, and Annotations to Both Versions

王永胜 李 艳 著
WANG Yong-sheng, LI Yan

哈尔滨工业大学出版社

内容提要

当前,在中西方文化交流日益繁盛以及"文化自信"和"一带一路"的背景之下,国内外学者对中国古诗词的翻译和研究方兴未艾。本书是《唐代五绝品读与英译研究及韵体英译探索》(上、下卷)中相关内容的延伸(可以算作其"姊妹篇"),重点对101首唐代五绝进行韵译方面的探索,并对五绝原诗及其译诗加注,以方便读者理解。本书对中国传统文化的国际传播具有现实意义。

本书共十三章,主要内容包括离别、乡情、友情、闲适、怨情、思恋、景色、物象、饮酒、月夜、哲思、悲秋以及边塞等类别的五绝及其韵体英译诗。

本书适合高等学校英语专业本科生及研究生阅读、参考,也可供感兴趣的非英语专业的本科生及研究生参考。本书也适合广大海内外文学爱好者阅读,更适合有关诗歌(特别是汉语古体诗和英文格律诗)和翻译等方面的学习者和研究者阅读、参考。

图书在版编目(CIP)数据

唐代五绝101首及其韵体英译并注/王永胜,李艳著.—哈尔滨:哈尔滨工业大学出版社,2019.4
ISBN 978-7-5603-4035-7

Ⅰ.①唐… Ⅱ.①王… ②李… Ⅲ.①唐诗–五言绝句–英语–文学翻译–研究 Ⅳ.①I207.227.42 ②H315.9
中国版本图书馆CIP数据核字(2019)第038713号

责任编辑	田新华
封面设计	刘长友
出版发行	哈尔滨工业大学出版社
社　　址	哈尔滨市南岗区复华四道街10号　邮编150006
传　　真	0451–86414749
网　　址	http://hitpress.hit.edu.cn
印　　刷	哈尔滨市道外区铭忆印刷厂
开　　本	880mm×1230mm　1/32　印张6.75　字数216千字
版　　次	2019年4月第1版　2019年4月第1次印刷
书　　号	ISBN 978-7-5603-4035-7
定　　价	45.00元

(如因印装质量问题影响阅读,我社负责调换)

前　言

　　中国是一个诗歌的国度,也是一座诗歌的百花园,而唐代诗歌则是这座百花园中一朵朵娇艳之花。这些娇艳之花装点着中国诗歌的百花园,令其变得绚烂无比、美妙绝伦、经久不衰,从而使之鸟语花香、芳香四溢、生机盎然。在这里,从古体诗歌,如"忽如一夜春风来,千树万树梨花开"(岑参《白雪歌送武判官归京》),到近体诗歌,如"日暮乡关何处是,烟波江上使人愁"(崔颢《黄鹤楼》),再到发端期的词作,如"思悠悠,恨悠悠,恨到归时方始休"(白居易《长相思·汴水流》),朵朵唐代诗歌("词"其实是一种特殊形式的"诗")之花争奇斗艳,令人目不暇接。

　　唐诗的美以及唐诗所表达的情感,无处不在。这里有依依惜别之情——"劝君更尽一杯酒,西出阳关无故人"(王维《渭城曲》,一作《送元二使安西》),"别离在今晨,见尔当何秋"(韦应物《送杨氏女》),"日暮酒醒人已远,满天风雨下西楼"(许浑《谢亭送别》),"醉不成欢惨将别,别时茫茫江浸月"(白居易《琵琶行》,一作《琵琶引》),"朝朝送别泣花钿,折尽春风杨柳烟"(鱼玄机《折杨柳·朝朝送别泣花钿》);这里有无尽的乡愁——"举头望明月,低头思故乡"(李白《静夜思》),"遥怜故园菊,应傍战场开"(岑参《行军九日思长安故园》),"此夜曲中闻折柳,何人不起故园情"(李白《春夜洛城闻笛》),"今夜月明人尽望,不知秋思落谁家"(王建《十五夜望月寄杜郎中》);这里有别后的思念——"愿君多采撷,此物最相思"(王维《相思》),"忆君心似西江水,日夜东流无歇时"(鱼玄机《江陵愁望寄子安》,一作《江陵愁望有寄》),"遥知兄弟登高处,遍插茱萸少一人"(王维《九月九日忆山东兄弟》),"花红易衰似郎意,水流无限似侬愁"(刘禹锡《竹枝词九首》其二),"啼时惊妾梦,不得到辽西"(金昌绪《春怨》,一作《伊州歌》);这里有对春的咏叹——"畏老身全老,逢春解惜春。今年看花伴,已少去年人"(李益《惜春伤同幕故人孟郎中兼呈去年看花友》),"无计延春日,何能驻少年"(杜牧《惜春》),"昨夜闲潭梦落花,可怜春半不还家"(张若虚《春江花月夜》),"残阳寂寞东城去,惆怅春风落尽花"(武元衡《崔敷叹春物将谢恨不同览时余方为事牵束及往寻不遇题之留赠》),"恰似春风相欺得,夜来吹折数枝花"(杜甫《绝句漫兴九首》其二);这里有真挚的劝勉话语——"莫愁前路无知己,天下谁人不识君"(高适《别董大二首》其一),"莫学武陵人,暂游桃源里"(裴迪《送崔九》,一作《崔九欲往南山马上口号与别》),"十年未称平生意,好得辛勤漫读书"(刘长卿《客舍喜郑三见寄》),"青春须早为,岂能长少年"(孟郊《劝学》),等等。这里有的,实在太多、太多,不胜枚举。徜徉在这座百花园中,真是令人流连忘返,犹入桃花源地,久久不肯离去。

君不见"茂陵刘郎秋风客,夜闻马嘶晓无迹"(李贺《金铜仙人辞汉歌》),却又是"闲云潭影日悠悠,物换星移几度秋"(王勃《滕王阁诗》)。是啊,物是人非。可是,时间是永恒的,那夜空中皎洁的明月是永恒的——"今人不见古时月,今月曾经照古人。"(李白《把酒问月·故人贾淳令予问之》)于是,唐代之后的一位文人不禁发出这样的感慨:"但愿人长久,千里共婵娟"(宋代苏轼《水调歌头·明月几时有》)。随着时间的推移,几乎一切都将化作历史的尘烟,那情景犹如"南朝四百八十寺,多少楼台烟雨中"(杜牧《江南春绝句》)。但是,诗永恒,这也是令人欣慰之事。在中国诗歌的百花园中,朵朵唐诗的娇艳之花,依然开放,吐露馨香。

在此,不妨将镜头拉近,你就会发现,在中国诗歌百花园里朵朵娇艳的唐诗之花中,有一种不起眼的小花,也在迎风绽开笑脸。虽小,却不孤单,却也娇艳,却也翩翩,却也非凡,且更为耀眼。这种小花,对唐诗的园区加以装点,令其更加辉煌、璀璨。这就是唐诗中的五绝——五言绝句。有谁不知道"春眠不觉晓,处处闻啼鸟",有谁不感叹"夜来风雨声,花落知多少",有谁不熟谙"红豆生南国,春来发几枝",又有谁不知道"欲穷千里目,更上一层楼!""白日依山尽,黄河入海流"的壮美,"千山鸟飞绝,万径人踪灭"的静谧,"一声何满子,双泪落君前"的幽怨,"落花如有意,来去逐船流"的情思,"古调虽自爱,今人多不弹"的悲叹……这一切的一切,又有谁没有体会过!

一般来说,所谓"五绝"应为"五言绝句"的省称,而"五言绝句"则为"五言律诗"的一半,即诗体四行且每行五言,所以五绝具有狭义性,专指"五言律绝"(从这个层面上讲,"五绝"实质上也是"五言律绝"的省称),而非"五言古绝"(其省称应为"五古绝")的省称①。但是,一提到"绝句",自然要提到"古绝"与"律绝",则"绝句"具有广义性:

> 古绝即古体诗的绝句,律绝指通常称为五绝、七绝的格律诗中的绝句。古绝与律绝,在体裁上的区别,突出表现在选择韵脚和讲究平仄这两个方面。
>
> 古绝的韵脚可押平声的也可押仄声的[sic]②,而律绝只押平声韵,不押仄声韵。读绝句时,发现它用的是仄声韵,那就能断定它不是律绝。但遇到用平声韵的绝句,还要根据它讲究平仄的程度,才能决定[sic]它属于哪种绝句。
>
> 古绝一般只关心两个字的平仄,它要求诗中三、四句的句末字必须平仄相反。如李绅《古风二首(其二)》③"谁知盘中餐,粒粒皆辛苦"的"餐(平)"与"苦(仄)",太上隐者《答人》"山中无历日,寒尽不知年"的"日(仄)"与"年(平)"。律绝则对诗中的全部用字,都要讲究平仄。在五绝、七绝的平仄格式上,从头到尾,何字该用平声,何字该用仄声,都有明确规定,写得清楚明白。
>
> (文东,2015:362)

至于仄韵诗是否为格律诗,专家学者间还存在着争议。目前有

---

① 更多关于"五绝"和"五古绝"方面的知识,敬请参阅本书上卷第五章第一节"五绝和五古绝"。

② "sic",拉丁文,意为"原文如此"。

③ 括号及括号内文字为本书著者所加。

很多专家学者认为符合格律要求的仄韵诗也是律诗,本书从之。另外,在历代唐诗选本中,不少选本将某些古绝特别是押仄韵的古绝视作律绝。具体体现,就是将某些五古绝归入五绝之列。鉴于此,为研究方便起见,本书中五绝作品的选取并不是严格限定在律绝上,而是在实际选取过程中将少量按严格要求应为五古绝的作品也选来,并采取某些唐诗选本的观点视其为五绝作品。简而言之,本书中所提取的具有代表性的唐代五绝作品,绝大多数为"律绝",个别为"古绝",具体为"五古绝",因这样的古绝在很多唐诗选本中又作五绝处置,故本书从之。

短小精悍的五绝,在理解其诗意之前,关键环节在于读懂,读懂的关键在于对字面含义的理解。读懂了,方可将其拿来与世人共赏,就是将中国传统文化传播到全世界。于是,鉴于英语的全球化特点,英译恐怕是其中一个主要的途径了。将唐代五绝这种小花拿来与世人共赏前,也就是在英译之前,要考虑到诸多的因素,如英诗格律、古诗英译目前所存在的各种状态等。其中,最主要的是要考虑一下英诗格律,特别是在把唐代五绝这样的古诗译成韵体英诗的情况之下,更得简单了解一下英诗的格律特点(详见《唐代五绝品读与英译研究及韵体英译探索》上卷)。正所谓"知彼知己,百战不殆;不知彼而知己,一败一负;不知彼不知己,每战必殆"[①]

在文化融合的大背景下,中国的古典诗歌要想走向世界,进入交流领域,英译是必然的一步。但是,古诗英译的难度很大,受到诸多因素的限制,也存在颇多的争议。例如,将古诗译成英语时,是译成英语的散文体、自由诗体、格律诗体,还是译成改写诗体形式,等等。所幸的是,不管是大家,还是小家,抑或后起之秀;不管是中国人,还

[①] 《孙子·谋攻篇》,转引自"付朝,2010:120"(全书类似引文格式仅注:读者可在书末参考文献姓名为付朝的作者于2010年出版的那本书的120页上找到)。

是外国人,抑或外籍华人,都对此做出了不懈的努力和探索,也为本书奠定了坚实的基础(详见《唐代五绝品读与英译研究及韵体英译探索》上卷)。

英诗,特别是古典英诗,在长期的演变过程中形成了一套类似汉语近体诗即格律诗的"格律"——音步、节奏、押韵等。如:

Let us then be up and doing,　我们站起来开始采取行动吧,
With a heart for any fate;　胸怀赤诚之心何惧命运好坏;
Still achieving, still pursuing,　仍然要进取和追求啊,
Learn to labor and to wait.　还要学会苦干和等待[①]。

这样,了解了英诗的格律,就可以"以诗译诗",也就是所谓诗歌的"移植",即韵体英译,简称"韵译"——本书研究的主题。当然,包括唐代五绝在内的古诗,也可以译成自由体英诗,或者散文体英文形式,或者改写体形式,对此国内外译者都做出了数量可观的尝试和探索。

本书在对唐代五绝进行简单分类的基础上,提取具有代表性的唐代五绝作品(绝大多数为"律绝",个别为"古绝",具体为"五古绝",但这样的五古绝在很多唐诗选本中又作五绝处置,故本书从之),共计101首,对其适当加注(汉语),做韵体英译探索,并对韵体英译诗加注(英汉对照加注形式)以便于读者把握和理解韵体英译诗的字面意义。对这些唐代五绝及其韵体英译诗所做的加注处理,重点放在两种版本诗歌的字面含义,不做过多引申,旨在使读者可以从不同的角度和层面最终理解并欣赏唐代五绝的精妙之处和意境之美,以及韵体英译诗的绝妙之处和意境之美(实际不一定如此,却是

---

① 亨利·沃兹沃斯·朗费罗(Henry Wadsworth Longfellow)《人生颂歌》(*A Psalm of Life*)节选,王永胜译。

著者追求的目标），以达传播中国文化之目的。与此同时，冒昧地希望这样的研究方式会收到"抛砖引玉"之功效，达到"举一反三"之效果。

　　需要说明的是，首先，为了给那些不能从头至尾阅读本书的读者一个完整的印象，更是为了方便读者阅读，本书中有些"注释"中的条目做了重复化处理。也就是说，为了那些"查找式"阅读者的需要，有些注释的条目反复再现，而未给出"Cross Reference"（交叉引用条目），以免除读者来回"参见"之苦。其次，书中所引原文（指放在引号中的原封不动的引用），为尊重原文内容及原文作者，除了个别处加括注、脚注或加"[sic]"（方括号中的内容为拉丁文，意为"原文如此"）字样标注外，一律原封不动对原文加以抄录。另外，书中所引的某些汉语原诗由于版本不一，最终采用的版本都有所说明或标明了出处。

　　本书不当之处，在所难免；错谬疏失，定当百出。敬请斧正，不吝赐教！

王永胜　李艳
2018年11月30日

目 录

第一章 离别五绝
Chapter 01 About Farewell ……………………………… 1

■ 001 :: ………………………………………………………… 1
 山中送别 ……………………………………………… 1
 □王维 ………………………………………………… 1
 Seeing off a Close Friend ……………………………… 2
  ○By WANG Wei …………………………………… 2

■ 002 :: ………………………………………………………… 2
 送灵澈上人 …………………………………………… 2
 □刘长卿 ……………………………………………… 2
 Parting with My Friend Lingche, an Honorable Monk …… 3
  ○By LIU Chang-qing ……………………………… 3

■ 003 :: ………………………………………………………… 4
 送崔九 ………………………………………………… 4
 □裴迪 ………………………………………………… 4
 Wishes before Bidding a Farewell to CUI Jiu, My Dear Friend … 4
  ○By PEI Di ………………………………………… 4

■ 004 :: ………………………………………………………… 5
 南浦别 ………………………………………………… 5
 □白居易 ……………………………………………… 5
 Parting with a Friend to the Southern River Bank ……… 6
  ○By BAI Ju-yi …………………………………… 6

■ 005 :: ………………………………………………………… 6

于易水送人 ··· 6
□骆宾王 ·· 6
A Feeling from Seeing off a Friend to Yishui River Bank ······· 7
○By LUO Bin-wang ·· 7

■ 006 :: ·· 8
南行别弟 ·· 8
□韦承庆 ·· 8
Parting with My Bro upon My Banishment from the Capital to
the South by Crossing the Yangtze River ················· 8
○By WEI Cheng-qing ······································ 8

■ 007 :: ·· 9
送苏尚书赴益州 ··· 9
□郑惟忠 ·· 9
Thoughts on a Farewell to Minister Su on His Way to Yizhou ··· 9
○By ZHENG Wei-zhong ···································· 9

■ 008 :: ·· 11
江亭夜月送别二首(其二) ··································· 11
□王勃 ·· 11
Moonlit Night Feelings from Seeing off Friends in the Riverside
Tower (Second of Two Poems with the Same Title) ········ 11
○By WANG Bo ··· 11

第二章　乡情五绝
Chapter 02　About Homesickness ···························· 13

■ 009 :: ·· 13
静夜思 ·· 13
□李白 ·· 13
Random Musing on a Silent Moonlit Night ··············· 14
○By LI Bai ··· 14

■ 010 :: ·· 15

渡汉江 ………………………………………………… 15
□宋之问 ………………………………………………… 15
Homesickness Prior to and after Crossing Hanjiang River …… 15
○By SONG Zhi-wen ………………………………… 15

■ 011 :: …………………………………………………… 16
杂诗 ……………………………………………………… 16
□王维 …………………………………………………… 16
A Poem about an Occasional Homesickness ……………… 17
○By WANG Wei ……………………………………… 17

■ 012 :: …………………………………………………… 18
滞雨 ……………………………………………………… 18
□李商隐 ………………………………………………… 18
A Raining Night in Chang'an …………………………… 18
○By LI Shang-yin …………………………………… 18

■ 013 :: …………………………………………………… 19
行军九日思长安故园 …………………………………… 19
□岑参 …………………………………………………… 19
Missing My Wartime Home Chang'an at Chongyang Festival … 20
○By CEN Shen ……………………………………… 20

■ 014 :: …………………………………………………… 21
关山月二首(其一) …………………………………… 21
□戴叔伦 ………………………………………………… 21
Sentimental Feelings upon Seeing the Moon over the Mountain
Pass (First of Two Poems with the Same Title) …………… 22
○By DAI Shu-lun …………………………………… 22

■ 015 :: …………………………………………………… 23
西过渭州见渭水思秦川 ………………………………… 23
□岑参 …………………………………………………… 23
The Sight of Weishui River Makes Me Think of Chang'an,

My Hometown in Qinchuan or Yongzhou, While Traveling West through Weizhou 24
　○By CEN Shen 24
　■ 016 :: 25
　绝句二首(其二) 25
　□杜甫 25
　Two Quatrains with Five Chinese Characters to Each Line (Second of Two Poems with the Same Title) 26
　○By DU Fu 26

第三章　友情五绝
Chapter 03　About Friendship 27
　■ 017 :: 27
　秋夜寄丘员外 27
　□韦应物 27
　An Autumn Night Poem to My Friend QIU Dan, an Extra Vice-minister 28
　○By WEI Ying-wu 28
　■ 018 :: 28
　相思 28
　□王维 28
　Red Berries 29
　○By WANG Wei 29
　■ 019 :: 29
　问刘十九 29
　□白居易 29
　A Question to LIU Shi-jiu, a Friend of Mine 30
　○By BAI Ju-yi 30
　■ 020 :: 30
　留卢秦卿 30

□司空曙 ……………………………………………… 30
Stay, LU Qin-qing, My Old Friend ………………… 31
○By SIKONG Shu ………………………………… 31

■ 021 :: …………………………………………………… 32
答陆澧 ……………………………………………… 32
□张九龄 …………………………………………… 32
Reply to My Friend LU Li's Invitation to a Gathering ………… 32
○By ZHANG Jiu-ling ……………………………… 32

■ 022 :: …………………………………………………… 33
逢谢偃 ……………………………………………… 33
□高适 ……………………………………………… 33
Seeing Once Again XIE Yan, My Old Friend ……… 34
○By GAO Shi ……………………………………… 34

■ 023 :: …………………………………………………… 34
林塘怀友 …………………………………………… 34
□王勃 ……………………………………………… 34
Thinking of My Friend from Where I Live in Seclusion ……… 35
○By WANG Bo …………………………………… 35

■ 024 :: …………………………………………………… 36
送朱大入秦 ………………………………………… 36
□孟浩然 …………………………………………… 36
Parting with ZHU Da, My Dear Friend Who Leaves for Chang'an in Qin Region ……………………………………… 36
○By MENG Hao-ran ……………………………… 36

第四章 闲适五绝
Chapter 04　About Unrestrainedness ………………… 38

■ 025 :: …………………………………………………… 38
江雪 ………………………………………………… 38
□柳宗元 …………………………………………… 38

An Angler in Snow ·················· 39
　○By LIU Zong-yuan ·················· 39
■ 026 :: ·················· 39
　寻隐者不遇 ·················· 39
　□贾岛 ·················· 39
　A Visit of the Recluse Only to Find He Is Absent ········· 40
　　○By JIA Dao ·················· 40
■ 027 :: ·················· 41
　春晓 ·················· 41
　□孟浩然 ·················· 41
　At Dawn of a Spring Day ·················· 41
　　○By MENG Hao-ran ·················· 41
■ 028 :: ·················· 42
　登鹳雀楼 ·················· 42
　□王之涣 ·················· 42
　Upon Mounting the Stork Tower ·················· 43
　　○By WANG Zhi-huan ·················· 43
■ 029 :: ·················· 44
　答人 ·················· 44
　□太上隐者 ·················· 44
　Answer to Question "Who Are You?" ·················· 44
　　○By Supreme Recluse ·················· 44
■ 030 :: ·················· 45
　牧竖 ·················· 45
　□崔道融 ·················· 45
　A Boy Who Grazes Cattle ·················· 45
　　○By CUI Dao-rong ·················· 45
■ 031 :: ·················· 47
　听山鹧鸪 ·················· 47

□顾况 ··· 47
　　While Enjoying the Music "Mountain Partridge" by Residents
　　of Peach Blossom Village ······························ 47
　　　○By GU Kuang ······································ 47
■ 032 :: ··· 48
　　钓叟 ··· 48
　　□杜荀鹤 ··· 48
　　An Aged Angler's Life ································· 49
　　　○By DU Xun-he ····································· 49

第五章　怨情五绝
Chapter 05　About Feelings of Resentment ············· 51
■ 033 :: ··· 51
　　怨情 ··· 51
　　□李白 ··· 51
　　A Feeling of Resentment ······························· 52
　　　○By LI Bai ··· 52
■ 034 :: ··· 53
　　春怨 ··· 53
　　□金昌绪 ··· 53
　　A Springtime Feeling of Resentment ···················· 53
　　　○By JIN Chang-xu ·································· 53
■ 035 :: ··· 54
　　江南曲 ··· 54
　　□李益 ··· 54
　　A Folk Song of Southern Yangtze River ················· 55
　　　○By LI Yi ·· 55
■ 036 :: ··· 56
　　何满子 ··· 56
　　□张祜 ··· 56

He Man-zi ·· 57
　　○By ZHANG Hu ··· 57
■ 037 :: ·· 58
　怨诗 ··· 58
　　□孟郊 ··· 58
　Song of a Lady's Lovesickness – based Resentment toward Her
　Long-time-no-see Husband ································ 59
　　○By MENG Jiao ·· 59
■ 038 :: ·· 59
　啰唝曲六首（其五） ······································· 59
　　□刘采春 ··· 59
　Luohong Tune：Songs of a Wife's Longing for the Return of
　Her Husband（Fifth of Six Poems with the Same Title）········ 60
　　○By LIU Cai-chun ······································ 60
■ 039 :: ·· 61
　春闺怨 ··· 61
　　□杜荀鹤 ··· 61
　A Lady's Sentimental Feelings in Spring ···················· 61
　　○By DU Xun-he ·· 61
■ 040 :: ·· 62
　闺怨二首（其一） ··· 62
　　□沈如筠 ··· 62
　A Wife's Longing for Her Husband Serving in the Southern
　Frontier（First of Two Poems with the Same Title）·········· 62
　　○By SHEN Ru-jun ······································ 62

第六章　思恋五绝
Chapter 06　About Longing for Love ························· 64
■ 041 :: ·· 64
　赋得自君之出矣 ··· 64

□张九龄 ………………………………………… 64
A Poem by Imitating Similar Poems with "Since You Left Me
for Your Career" as Their First Line ………………… 65
　○By ZHANG Jiu-ling ………………………………… 65

■ 042 :: ……………………………………………… 65
鹧鸪词 …………………………………………………… 65
□李益 …………………………………………………… 65
A Poem Aroused by Sentimental Songs of Partridges ………… 66
　○By LI Yi ……………………………………………… 66

■ 043 :: ……………………………………………… 67
江南曲 …………………………………………………… 67
□储光羲 ………………………………………………… 67
A Folk Song of Southern Yangtze River ………………… 68
　○By CHU Guang-xi …………………………………… 68

■ 044 :: ……………………………………………… 69
听筝 ……………………………………………………… 69
□李端 …………………………………………………… 69
Listening to Melody on Zheng, a Zither-like 12-to-21-
string Traditional Chinese Instrument ………………… 70
　○By LI Duan ………………………………………… 70

■ 045 :: ……………………………………………… 72
春闺思 …………………………………………………… 72
□张仲素 ………………………………………………… 72
A Madam's Fond Spring Memory of Her Husband Serving
in Yuyang, the Frontier ………………………………… 72
　○By ZHANG Zhong-su ……………………………… 72

■ 046 :: ……………………………………………… 74
题玉泉溪 ………………………………………………… 74
□湘驿女子 ……………………………………………… 74

A Mysterious Story from Jade Fountain Brook ………………… 75
　　○By Lady Xiangyi ………………………………………… 75
■ 047 :: ……………………………………………………… 76
　大酺乐 ……………………………………………………… 76
　□张文收 …………………………………………………… 76
　"Dapu Music": Song of a Lady's Wishful Longing for Seeing
　Her Beloved ………………………………………………… 77
　　○By ZHANG Wen-shou ………………………………… 77
■ 048 :: ……………………………………………………… 78
　江南曲五首(其一) ………………………………………… 78
　□丁仙芝 …………………………………………………… 78
　A Folk Song of Southern Yangtze River by a Vivacious
　Girl (First of Five Poems with the Same Title) …………… 78
　　○By DING Xian-zhi …………………………………… 78

第七章　景色五绝
Chapter 07　About Scenery ……………………………… 80
■ 049 :: ……………………………………………………… 80
　鹿柴 ………………………………………………………… 80
　□王维 ……………………………………………………… 80
　In Luzhai, One of the Scenic Spots Where I Live as a Recluse … 81
　　○By WANG Wei ………………………………………… 81
■ 050 :: ……………………………………………………… 82
　宿建德江 …………………………………………………… 82
　□孟浩然 …………………………………………………… 82
　Staying Overnight in My Boat Floating on Jiande River ……… 82
　　○By MENG Hao-ran …………………………………… 82
■ 051 :: ……………………………………………………… 84
　终南望余雪 ………………………………………………… 84
　□祖咏 ……………………………………………………… 84

目录

A Fine View of Lingering Snow on Top of Zhongnan Mountain ··· 85
　○By ZU Yong ·· 85
■ 052 :: ·· 86
行宫 ··· 86
□元稹 ·· 86
The Imperial Palace for Emperor's Temporary Needs ············ 87
　○By YUAN Zhen ·· 87
■ 053 :: ·· 88
乐游原 ·· 88
□李商隐 ·· 88
A Tour in My Carriage to Leyouyuan ························· 88
　○By LI Shang-yin ··· 88
■ 054 :: ·· 90
长安秋望 ·· 90
□杜牧 ·· 90
Looking Afar at Chang'an in Autumn ························ 90
　○By DU Mu ··· 90
■ 055 :: ·· 92
江村夜泊 ·· 92
□项斯 ·· 92
The Scenery of a Riverside Village I Observed at Night after
Mooring by It ·· 92
　○By XIANG Si ·· 92
■ 056 :: ·· 93
春游曲二首(其一) ··· 93
□王涯 ·· 93
Songs of Outings in Spring (First of Two Poems with the Same
Title) ·· 93
　○By WANG Ya ··· 93

第八章　物象五绝
Chapter 08　About Images of Object ········ 95

■ 057 :: ·· 95
　曲池荷 ··· 95
　□卢照邻 ·· 95
　Lotus on Qujiang Pond ························ 96
　○By LU Zhao-lin ································ 96

■ 058 :: ·· 97
　宫槐陌 ··· 97
　□裴迪 ··· 97
　The Acacia Tree-lined Lane ·················· 98
　○By PEI Di ·· 98

■ 059 :: ·· 98
　春雪 ··· 98
　□刘方平 ·· 98
　An Ironical Thought on Snow in Spring ··· 99
　○By LIU Fang-ping ······························ 99

■ 060 :: ·· 100
　落叶 ··· 100
　□孔绍安 ·· 100
　The Falling of the Leaf ······················· 100
　○By KONG Shao-an ··························· 100

■ 061 :: ·· 101
　风 ·· 101
　□李峤 ··· 101
　The Wind ··· 102
　○By LI Qiao ····································· 102

■ 062 :: ·· 103

| 江边柳 ··· 103
| □雍裕之 ·· 103
| The Riverside Willows ····························· 103
| ○By YONG Yu-zhi ································ 103
■ 063 :: ·· 104
| 沙上鹭 ··· 104
| □张文姬 ·· 104
| The Heron Standing on the Sand ················ 105
| ○By ZHANG Wen-ji ······························· 105
■ 064 :: ·· 106
| 山下泉 ··· 106
| □皇甫曾 ·· 106
| A Flow of Water after Running Down the Mountain ········ 106
| ○By HUANGFU Zeng ······························ 106

第九章 饮酒五绝
Chapter 09　About Drinking ················· 107
■ 065 :: ·· 107
| 过酒家五首(其二) ··································· 107
| □王绩 ··· 107
| Ironical Thoughts while Drinking in a Pub (Second of Five
| Poems with the Same Title) ······················· 108
| ○By WANG Ji ·· 108
■ 066 :: ·· 109
| 偶游主人园 ·· 109
| □贺知章 ·· 109
| Travels to the Garden at Times ·················· 109
| ○By HE Zhi-zhang ·································· 109
■ 067 :: ·· 110
| 闲居 ·· 110

· 13 ·

□高适 …… 110
While Living in a Carefree Way …… 111
　○By GAO Shi …… 111
■ 068 :: …… 112
江楼 …… 112
□杜牧 …… 112
On the Riverside Tower …… 112
　○By DU Mu …… 112
■ 069 :: …… 113
劝酒 …… 113
□于武陵 …… 113
Urging You to Drink …… 114
　○By YU Wu-ling …… 114
■ 070 :: …… 115
招东邻 …… 115
□白居易 …… 115
An Invitation to My Eastern Neighbour for a Drink …… 115
　○By BAI Ju-yi …… 115
■ 071 :: …… 116
三月晦日送客 …… 116
□崔橹 …… 116
Wishes before Bidding a Farewell to My Friend at the Ending of Spring …… 117
　○By CUI Lu …… 117
■ 072 :: …… 118
劝陆三饮酒 …… 118
□戴叔伦 …… 118
Urging My Friend LU San to Drink …… 118
　○By DAI Shu-lun …… 118

第十章 月夜五绝
Chapter 10　About Moonlit Nights
- 073 :: ……………………………………………… 120
  - 中秋月二首(其二) ………………………………… 120
  - □李峤 …………………………………………… 120
  - Full Moon of Mid-autumn Festival Night (Second of Two Poems with the Same Title) …………………… 121
    - ○By LI Qiao ………………………………… 121
- 074 :: ……………………………………………… 121
  - 拜新月 …………………………………………… 121
  - □李端 …………………………………………… 121
  - Praying to the Crescent Moon ………………… 122
    - ○By LI Duan ………………………………… 122
- 075 :: ……………………………………………… 123
  - 玉台体十二首(其十) ……………………………… 123
  - □权德舆 ………………………………………… 123
  - Yutai-style Love Poetry (Tenth of Twelve Poems with the Same Title) ……………………………………… 123
    - ○By QUAN De-yu …………………………… 123
- 076 :: ……………………………………………… 125
  - 芦花 ……………………………………………… 125
  - □雍裕之 ………………………………………… 125
  - Reed Spikes …………………………………… 125
    - ○By YONG Yu-zhi ………………………… 125
- 077 :: ……………………………………………… 126
  - 送郭司仓 ………………………………………… 126
  - □王昌龄 ………………………………………… 126
  - A Feeling from Seeing off Mr. Guo with Sicang as His Official Title …………………………………………… 127

○ By WANG Chang-ling ······ 127
■ 078 :: ······ 128
清溪泛舟 ······ 128
□张旭 ······ 128
A Boat Trip through the Limpid Stream ······ 129
○ By ZHANG Xu ······ 129
■ 079 :: ······ 129
清夜酌 ······ 129
□张说 ······ 129
Drinking Carefree at Moonlit Night ······ 130
○ By ZHANG Yue ······ 130
■ 080 :: ······ 131
小院 ······ 131
□唐彦谦 ······ 131
In the Small Yard during the Night ······ 131
○ By TANG Yan-qian ······ 131

第十一章 哲思五绝
Chapter 11 About Philosophical Thinking ······ 133

■ 081 :: ······ 133
蝉 ······ 133
□虞世南 ······ 133
The Cicada ······ 134
○ By YU Shi-nan ······ 134
■ 082 :: ······ 135
鸟鸣涧 ······ 135
□王维 ······ 135
The Ravine above Which a Bird's Chirp Rings ······ 135
○ By WANG Wei ······ 135
■ 083 :: ······ 136

溪口云 ……………………………………………… 136
□张文姬 …………………………………………… 136
The Cloud above the Stream …………………… 137
○By ZHANG Wen-ji ……………………………… 137

■ 084 :: ……………………………………………… 137
小松 ………………………………………………… 137
□王建 ……………………………………………… 137
A Pine-tree Sapling ……………………………… 137
○By WANG Jian …………………………………… 137

■ 085 :: ……………………………………………… 138
放鱼 ………………………………………………… 138
□李群玉 …………………………………………… 138
Advice to the Captive Fish Who Is to Be Set Free ………… 139
○By LI Qun-yu …………………………………… 139

■ 086 :: ……………………………………………… 140
幽居乐 ……………………………………………… 140
□施肩吾 …………………………………………… 140
My Single-minded Leisure to Live in Seclusion ………… 140
○By SHI Jian-wu ………………………………… 140

■ 087 :: ……………………………………………… 141
退居漫题七首（其七）……………………………… 141
□司空图 …………………………………………… 141
Random Thoughts while Living in Seclusion（Seventh of Seven Poems with the Same Title）………… 141
○By SIKONG Tu ………………………………… 142

第十二章 悲秋五绝
Chapter 12 About Autumnal Unpleasantness ………… 143

■ 088 :: ……………………………………………… 143
汾上惊秋 …………………………………………… 143

□苏颋 ……………………………………………… 143
A Surprise Sight of Autumnal View along the Fenshui River …… 144
○By SU Ting ……………………………………… 144

089 ::…………………………………………… 145
秋日 ………………………………………………… 145
□耿湋 ……………………………………………… 145
On an Autumn Day ……………………………… 145
○By GENG Wei …………………………………… 145

090 ::…………………………………………… 146
伤秋 ………………………………………………… 146
□钱起 ……………………………………………… 146
The Autumnal Sadness …………………………… 146
○By QIAN Qi ……………………………………… 146

091 ::…………………………………………… 147
立秋前一日览镜 …………………………………… 147
□李益 ……………………………………………… 147
Thoughts while Looking in the Mirror One Day before the
Beginning of Autumn …………………………… 148
○By LI Yi ………………………………………… 148

092 ::…………………………………………… 149
蜀道后期 …………………………………………… 149
□张说 ……………………………………………… 149
My Late Return to Luoyang City, My Hometown, from the
Region of Shu …………………………………… 149
○By ZHANG Yue ………………………………… 149

093 ::…………………………………………… 151
玉台体十二首（其九） …………………………… 151
□权德舆 …………………………………………… 151
Yutai-style Love Poetry (Ninth of Twelve Poems with the

Same Title) ⋯⋯⋯⋯⋯⋯⋯⋯⋯⋯⋯⋯⋯⋯⋯⋯⋯ 151
○By QUAN De-yu ⋯⋯⋯⋯⋯⋯⋯⋯⋯⋯⋯⋯⋯ 151

■ 094 ∷ ⋯⋯⋯⋯⋯⋯⋯⋯⋯⋯⋯⋯⋯⋯⋯⋯⋯⋯⋯ 153
中秋 ⋯⋯⋯⋯⋯⋯⋯⋯⋯⋯⋯⋯⋯⋯⋯⋯⋯⋯⋯⋯ 153
□司空图 ⋯⋯⋯⋯⋯⋯⋯⋯⋯⋯⋯⋯⋯⋯⋯⋯⋯⋯ 153
On the Mid-autumn Night ⋯⋯⋯⋯⋯⋯⋯⋯⋯ 153
○By SIKONG Tu ⋯⋯⋯⋯⋯⋯⋯⋯⋯⋯⋯⋯⋯⋯ 153

第十三章 边塞五绝
Chapter 13 About Frontier Warfare ⋯⋯⋯⋯⋯ 155

■ 095 ∷ ⋯⋯⋯⋯⋯⋯⋯⋯⋯⋯⋯⋯⋯⋯⋯⋯⋯⋯⋯ 155
和张仆射塞下曲六首(其三) ⋯⋯⋯⋯⋯⋯⋯⋯ 155
□卢纶 ⋯⋯⋯⋯⋯⋯⋯⋯⋯⋯⋯⋯⋯⋯⋯⋯⋯⋯ 155
Poetry by Imitating Rhyming Style of "Ode to Frontier Warfare" by Mr. Zhang, General Manager of Officials (Third of Six Poems with the Same Title) ⋯⋯⋯⋯⋯⋯⋯⋯⋯⋯⋯⋯ 156
○By LU Lun ⋯⋯⋯⋯⋯⋯⋯⋯⋯⋯⋯⋯⋯⋯⋯ 156

■ 096 ∷ ⋯⋯⋯⋯⋯⋯⋯⋯⋯⋯⋯⋯⋯⋯⋯⋯⋯⋯⋯ 157
塞下 ⋯⋯⋯⋯⋯⋯⋯⋯⋯⋯⋯⋯⋯⋯⋯⋯⋯⋯⋯⋯ 157
□许浑 ⋯⋯⋯⋯⋯⋯⋯⋯⋯⋯⋯⋯⋯⋯⋯⋯⋯⋯ 157
Ode to Frontier Warfare ⋯⋯⋯⋯⋯⋯⋯⋯⋯⋯ 158
○By XU Hun ⋯⋯⋯⋯⋯⋯⋯⋯⋯⋯⋯⋯⋯⋯⋯ 158

■ 097 ∷ ⋯⋯⋯⋯⋯⋯⋯⋯⋯⋯⋯⋯⋯⋯⋯⋯⋯⋯⋯ 159
闺怨词三首(其三) ⋯⋯⋯⋯⋯⋯⋯⋯⋯⋯⋯⋯ 159
□白居易 ⋯⋯⋯⋯⋯⋯⋯⋯⋯⋯⋯⋯⋯⋯⋯⋯⋯ 159
A Wife's Deep Concern for Her Husband Serving in the Frontier (Third of Three Poems with the Same Title) ⋯⋯⋯ 160
○By BAI Ju-yi ⋯⋯⋯⋯⋯⋯⋯⋯⋯⋯⋯⋯⋯⋯ 160

■ 098 ∷ ⋯⋯⋯⋯⋯⋯⋯⋯⋯⋯⋯⋯⋯⋯⋯⋯⋯⋯⋯ 160
从军词五首(其二) ⋯⋯⋯⋯⋯⋯⋯⋯⋯⋯⋯⋯ 160

□令狐楚 ·· 160
Lines about Military Service on the Frontier (Second of Five Poems with the Same Title) ················· 161
○By LINGHU Chu ··· 161

■ 099 ∷ ··· 162
从军行 ·· 162
□王昌龄 ·· 162
Song of Frontier Warfare ································· 162
○By WANG Chang-ling ································· 162

■ 100 ∷ ··· 163
哥舒歌 ·· 163
□西鄙人 ·· 163
Song of General Geshu ································· 164
○By The Man from Northwestern Border of Tang Dynasty ··· 164

■ 101 ∷ ··· 165
马诗二十三首(其五) ····································· 165
□李贺 ·· 165
Poetry of Inward Thoughts of a Horse (Fifth of Twenty-three Poems with the Same Title) ················· 166
○By LI He ··· 166

参考文献 ·· 168
后记 ·· 182

第一章 离别五绝

Chapter 01 About Farewell

■ **001** ::

山中送别　□王维

山中相送罢，日暮掩柴扉。
春草明年绿，王孙归不归？

五绝原诗注释（Annotations to the Original Chinese Version）

这首五绝的题目为《山中送别》，是唐代大诗人王维（701—761）的作品。此诗诗题一作《送别》或《送友》，尾联出句"春草明年绿"中的"明年"，有的版本亦作"年年"。尾联对句"王孙归不归"中，"王孙"本来是指贵族的子孙，诗中指代诗人所送的友人。

这首诗构思非凡，颇具特色。不同于常规的离别之诗的地方，就在于诗人王维并未着笔于眼前的"离别"场景直抒胸臆，而是将时间向后做了推移处理，将离别画面置于诗意之外，着眼于未来，浓墨重彩于"送罢"的场景、行为以及希冀——盼望着，盼望着，盼望春草再绿时，能与友人再次相聚，共叙情怀。读罢更具苍凉之感，寂寞的心境被诗人烘托得微妙而真挚。全诗语言朴实、情感自然、思绪高远，很具真情实感，耐人寻味，令人仿佛置身离别的现场。

Seeing off a Close Friend
○By *WANG Wei*

Havin' seen off my dear friend on th' mount track,
I shut my wooden door before th' day's black.
Suppose next spring grass has turn'd green—
"Would you, my friend, come again on the scene?"

Annotations to Its Version of English Verse（韵体译诗注释）①

1. havin' = having
2. th' = the
3. mount：*Noun* a mountain or hill（archaic except in place names）(除用于地名外均为古义) 山；丘
4. come/appear/arrive on the scene：arrive in/at a place, probably to change the existing situation 到达现场；露面；出现（或许会改变现存的局面）

002 ::

送灵澈上人　　□刘长卿
苍苍竹林寺，杳杳钟声晚。
荷笠带斜阳，青山独归远。

五绝原诗注释（Annotations to the Original Chinese Version）

这是唐代诗人刘长卿（约709~725—约786~791）的一首仄韵五言诗，当属律体绝句，即律绝，也就是五绝。当然，对此专家学者持有争议。虽然首句稍有"变格"，但仍可划归为五绝之列。对于押仄韵的诗算不算格律诗，确实存在一些争议。当然，浩如繁星的唐代格

---

① 韵体译诗的英汉双语注释部分，大多出自《新牛津英汉双解大词典》，但本书著者对其汉语部分做了不同程度的微调和修改；还有一些注释的英文部分出自一些网络版英文词典或百科全书，引入时本书著者做了编辑处理，但其汉语部分或由著者移植于某些汉语词典，或由著者翻译。上述所提注释的英文原文或汉语译文的具体出处，恕未一一列出，而是统一列入书后的"参考文献"中。

律诗绝大部分都押平韵。但是,也有一些诗人,其中不乏唐代的大家,写了一些仄韵诗。有些人干脆将这样的仄韵诗当作古体诗来看待。古体诗,通俗点儿说,就是古代的"自由体诗"。

《送灵澈上人》这首诗仿若一幅离别时的风景画,情谊融入画中,画中透出情与谊,既是离别诗的典范,又是山水诗的名篇。在这首诗中,看不到王维《山中送别》的孤寂和怅惘,看到的只是闲淡和雅致,这可能与诗人送别对象的身份有关吧。

Parting with My Friend Lingche, an Honorable Monk
○By *LIU Chang-qing*
Dark green *Zhulin* Temple in th' distance far
Rings with eve tolls as if from the bell jar.
Against the setting sun atop green hills,
A lone rain hat moves to th' Temple for miles.

N. B. Zhulin Temple：Located in southwestern part of today's Jiangsu Province, China, it is a Buddhist temple hidden among bamboo woods with green hills behind it. Here, *Zhulin* is a Chinese expression, meaning "bamboo woods".

Annotations to Its Version of English Verse（韵体译诗注释）

1. th' = the

2. ring：*Verb* (of a place) resound or reverberate with (a sound or sounds) (地方)响起;回响起

3. eve：*Noun* (chiefly poetic/literary) evening (主要为诗/文表达)黄昏;傍晚 (e.g. a bitter winter's eve 一个严冬的傍晚)

4. toll：*Noun* (in sing.) a single ring of a bell 一记钟声

5. bell jar：(figurative) an environment in which someone is protected or cut off from the outside world (比喻用法)与世隔绝的安乐窝;世外桃源

6. atop：*Preposition* on the top of... 在……顶上

7. lone：*Adjective* (attrib.) having no companions; solitary or single 单独的;孤独的;独自的

003 ::

送崔九　　□裴迪

归山深浅去,须尽丘壑美。

莫学武陵人,暂游桃源里。

五绝原诗注释(Annotations to the Original Chinese Version)

这是唐代诗人裴迪(约716—?)的一首五绝《送崔九》,一作《崔九欲往南山马上口号与别》。这是一首五言仄韵诗,但是,格律方面不很严谨,当属"五古绝"。考虑到它对格律方面的讲究程度,很多选本将其划为"五绝"之列。如蘅塘退士的《唐诗三百首》等很多选本都将此诗当作"五言绝句"处理,这当中考虑的恐怕是"拗救"的因素。本书从之,也将这首诗视作"五绝"。这首离别诗向读者呈现出一种静态之美。离别之前,静静对坐。"马上口号",即指骑坐于马背之上顺口吟成诗句,亦可谓相对"静坐"。归去之前,以言相劝,此乃"劝勉"式离别。

尾联出句里的"武陵人",指陶潜笔下《桃花源记》里的那个武陵渔人,他几经辗转进入桃花源地,却没过多长时间就出来了。

Wishes before Bidding a Farewell to CUI Jiu, My Dear Friend

○By *PEI Di*

'Mong th' hills an' vales since you have retreated,

Try to admire beauties you've been greeted.

Don't be such a tourist who chanced to run

Into Shangri-La but left with no fun.

Annotations to Its Version of English Verse(韵体译诗注释)

1. wish: *Noun* (usu. wishes) an expression of such a desire, typically in the form of a request or instruction 请求;要求 (e.g. She must carry out her late father's wishes. 她必须实现先父的遗愿。)

2. 'Mong = Among

3. th' = the

4. an' = and

5. vale: *Noun* a valley (used in place names or as a poetic term)（用于地名或作为诗歌术语）谷；溪谷

6. greet: *Verb* (of a sight or sound) become apparent to or be noticed by (someone) on arrival somewhere（景象或声音）呈现在……前；被……所感知

7. admire: *Verb* look at with pleasure 欣赏

8. chance: *Verb* (no obj. with infinitive) do something by accident or without design 偶然；碰巧

9. Shangri-La: *Noun* a place regarded as an earthly paradise, especially when involving a retreat from the pressures of modern civilization（人间的）理想乐园；世外桃源；香格里拉

004 ::

南浦别　□白居易
南浦凄凄别，西风袅袅秋。
一看肠一断，好去莫回头。

五绝原诗注释（Annotations to the Original Chinese Version）

在这首诗中，诗人白居易(772—846)细腻地刻画出送别、离别的生动景象。此诗以景起兴，转笔抒情，结句劝慰，层层深入地表达了诗人依依不舍的离别感伤情怀。"南浦"本来是指水的南边，或者南面的水滨，但也有真实的地名存在。比如今天的重庆市万州区，古时候名为"南浦"，是蜀汉建兴八年(公元230年)开始设置的一个县。后来，南浦就演变成一个送别的地点，成了古人水边送别的场所。

叠字往往会增添形象化的意象，比单字更有力、更感人。用好了，会十分形象、传神。此诗首联中，"凄凄"表达了离别之人内心的凄楚和愁苦，而"袅袅"更是渲染了秋天的凄凉和萧瑟，反衬了内心的"凄凄"。两组叠字遥相呼应，如泣如诉，离别之意顿时荡气回肠开来，读罢几乎就令人"腹中如汤灌，肝肠寸寸断"（《乐府诗集·华山畿二十五首》之一）了。

Parting with a Friend to the Southern River Bank
○By *BAI Ju-yi*
When we parted sad to the river bank,
The autumn wind kept blowing cold an' dank.
Looking to each other with broken hearts,
Into him I dinned "Going on" with lone darts.

N. B. Southern River Bank is usually the place for ancient Chinese people to sadly part with each other.

Annotations to Its Version of English Verse（韵体译诗注释）

1. an' = and

2. dank：*Adjective* disagreeably damp, cold, and musty 潮湿阴冷的

3. din：*Verb*（with obj.）(of a fact) be instilled in (someone) by constant repetition 对（某人）不停唠叨；反复叮嘱

4. dart：*Noun*（figurative）a sudden, intense pang of a particular emotion（比喻用法）一阵剧痛；一阵悲痛

005 ::

于易水送人　□骆宾王
此地别燕丹，壮士发冲冠。
昔时人已没，今日水犹寒。

五绝原诗注释（Annotations to the Original Chinese Version）

很多选本都将骆宾王（约638—约684）这首诗归为"五绝"的范畴，但是严格来说，排除"入声字"等因素，这首诗有"破格"和"失黏"之处，实为"五古绝"。考虑到这首诗整体上在平仄等方面的协调性，很多选本将其列为"五绝"体式，本书从之，将其视为"五绝"。关于此诗的标题，版本不一，说法不一。《全唐诗》卷79第40首载有此诗，题目为《于易水送人》，本书从之。但是，也有其他版本的标题，如《于易水送别》《于易水送人一绝》《易水送人》《易水送别》《易水》等。另外，也有个别选本将其首联的对句写成"壮发上冲冠"。

易水是一条河流的名称,位于今天的河北省境内,也称为易河,分为三部分:南易水、中易水和北易水。这条河流之所以名气十足,就是因为历史上的一段往事——燕太子丹(战国末年燕王喜的太子燕丹)送荆轲去刺杀秦王时,燕丹送荆轲于易水河畔.分手离别之际,荆轲怒发冲冠,伴随着高渐离击筑的节奏,高歌一曲,慷慨激昂地唱着《易水歌》,场面甚为雄伟、壮观。

A Feeling from Seeing off a Friend to Yishui River Bank
○By *LUO Bin-wang*

When Dan to JingK' bid farewell here,
The latter bristles with no fear.
Alas! They are heroes age-old,
But now the River still runs cold.

N. B. In the ancient Chinese Warring States Period (475 B. C.—221 B. C.), Prince *Dan* of the State of Yan finally chose *JingK'* (The complete spelling in Chinese *Pinyin* is "*Jing Ke*") and sent him as a hero to kill King *Ying Zheng* (who later became the first emperor in Chinese history, known as *Qin Shi-huang*) of the State of Qin, so as to protect his state from being conquered by the State of Qin. Before the action, Dan saw JingK' off to *Yishui River* (which is located in today's Hebei Province, a province in the northern part of China) bank, and *JingK'* showed his loyalty, devotion and fearlessness by singing "*Yishui Song*" before leaving for the killing, but failed in his action. Even so, this episode of Dan seeing *JingK'* off to Yishui River bank has become a historic legend, and hence the famous *Yishui River*, which has become a sad place in poetry for friends to part.

Annotations to Its Version of English Verse(韵体译诗注释)

1. bristle: *Verb* (no obj.) (of hair or fur) stand upright away from the skin, typically as a sign of anger or fear(毛发或皮毛)竖立

2. age-old: *Adjective* having existed for a very long time 存在很久的;古老的

3. alas: *Exclamation* (chiefly poetic literary or humorous) an expression of

grief, pity, or concern(主要用在诗文中,或者表示幽默)哎呀;唉(表示悲痛、遗憾或关心)

006 ::

南行别弟 □韦承庆

澹澹长江水,悠悠远客情。
落花相与恨,到地一无声。

五绝原诗注释(Annotations to the Original Chinese Version)

唐中宗神龙元年(公元705年),韦承庆(639—705)因攀附张易之而获罪,被贬至端州(今广东肇庆)任高要县尉。《南行别弟》作于韦承庆遭贬谪之际。当时,韦承庆与亲人分别,奔赴贬所。因高要在唐代都城长安南部,故曰"南行"。此诗也存在着作者之争,《全唐诗》崔道融名下录有此诗,诗题为《寄人二首》(其二)。

韦承庆《南行别弟》首联入对,但首句不入韵,用了两个叠音词。"澹澹"为水波缓缓晃动的样子,"悠悠"有绵长、久远之意。诗人赴贬所高要须跨过长江,故诗中提及"长江水";"远客"为诗人自称,因从西安至高要路途遥远。尾联意思是说"落花与我们同忧伤,坠落地上全无声响"(文东,2015:181)。另外,结句中的"一",一作"亦"。

Parting with My Bro upon My Banishment from the Capital to the South by Crossing the Yangtze River

○By *WEI Cheng-qing*

My stream of sadness flows far, far 'way,
As th' rippling river does night and day.
My bro and I hate th' mute parting hours,
The same way as the reluctant flowers
That hate to part with their stalk
Fall to the ground with no talk.

Annotations to Its Version of English Verse(韵体译诗注释)

1. bro: *Noun* (informal) short for brother(非正式用法)brother 的简称

2. banishment: *Noun* rejection by means of an act of banishing or proscribing someone 排斥；贬谪

3. Yangtze: *Noun* the principal river of China, which rises as the Jinsha in the Tibetan highlands and flows 6,380 km (3,964 miles) southwards then generally eastwards through central China, entering the East China Sea at Shanghai 扬子江；长江 (中国主要河流,发源于青藏高原的金沙江,全长6,380公里,即3,964英里,先向南流,后大致向东流,穿过中国中部,在上海流入中国东海)

4. 'way = away

5. th' = the

6. ripple: *Verb* (no obj.) (of water) form or flow with small waves on the surface (水)起涟漪；起微波

7. stalk: *Noun* the slender attachment or support of a leaf, flower, or fruit (叶、花或果实的)梗；柄；茎

007 ::

送苏尚书赴益州　□郑惟忠
离忧将岁尽,归望逐春来。
庭花如有意,留艳待人开。

五绝原诗注释（Annotations to the Original Chinese Version）

郑惟忠(？—723),唐时宋州宋城(今河南商丘)人。唐玄宗开元之初,郑惟忠为礼部尚书、太子宾客。《全唐诗》第45卷录其诗一首,即《送苏尚书赴益州》,一作《答苏尚书赴益州》(霍松林,1991：81)。

诗题中,"苏尚书"不可考,应为诗人一位苏姓朋友,任尚书一职；"益州"应为今成都一带地区。此诗首联入对,但首句不入韵。"离忧"意为离别的忧愁或忧思,"归望"是归家的愿望或希望。

Thoughts on a Farewell to Minister Su on His Way to Yizhou
○By ZHENG Wei-zhong

With slow ending of the year ends
My homesickness, and th' spring lends

A thread of hope to me, so that
I may go home, not feeling flat.
How I wish th' flowers in my grounds
'Pon my return bloomed with no bounds!

N. B. In the title of the translated poem, "Minister Su", a friend of the poet's, corresponds to "SU Shang-shu" (苏尚书) in the original poem, in which "Shang-shu" (approximately equivalent to "minister" in English) is a high official in ancient China and is usually used to follow the official's last name in ancient China to temporarily replace his/her first name (In Chinese name, the last name comes first, while the first name, last). "Yizhou" is a place name in ancient China, which is in today's Sichuan Province, and is centered around its capital city, Chengdu City.

Annotations to Its Version of English Verse (韵体译诗注释)

1. farewell: *Noun* an act of parting or of marking someone's departure 道别；告别；辞行；饯行 (e.g. The dinner had been arranged as a farewell. 安排这顿饭是为了饯行。)

2. homesickness: *Noun* a longing to return home 想家；思乡

3. th' = the

4. lend: *Verb* to impart or contribute (something, esp. some abstract quality) 给予；增添 (e.g. The dress lent charm to the girl. 那件衣服给那个姑娘增添了妩媚。)

5. flat: *Adjective* (of a person) without energy; dispirited (人) 没精打采的；颓废的；情绪低落的 (e.g. His sense of intoxication wore off until he felt flat and weary. 他的陶醉感渐渐消失，最终他感到没精打采、疲惫不堪。)

6. ground: *Noun* (grounds) an area of enclosed land surrounding a large house or other building (建筑物周围的) 场地；庭园 (e.g. The house stands in seven acres of grounds. 房子伫立在七英亩的庭园之中。)

7. 'Pon = Upon

8. bloom: *Verb* (no obj.) produce flowers; be in flower 开花；在开花；处于花期

9. bound: *Noun* a limitation or restriction on feeling or action 限制；限制范围（e.g. Enthusiasm to join the union knew no bounds. 人们加入该联盟的热情无限高涨。）

008 ::

江亭夜月送别二首（其二） □王勃
乱烟笼碧砌，飞月向南端。
寂寂离亭掩，江山此夜寒。

五绝原诗注释（Annotations to the Original Chinese Version）
"初唐四杰"之首的王勃（约650—约676），大约在旅居巴蜀期间写就这两首送客离别之作，即《江亭夜月送别二首》，本书选的是其中的第二首。此诗中，主要意象为江、亭、夜、月、烟、山等，描绘了一个月夜诗人在江边亭中送客离去的情景和感受。诗人将离别的孤寂之情融入景物之中，表达了诗人独特的离别感受。

此诗首联人对，但首句不入韵。"碧砌"为青绿色的石阶或青石台阶，"南端"当指"离亭的正南门"（霍松林，1991：35）。晋代潘岳《悼亡诗》云："皎皎窗中月，照我室南端"，唐代李善对此注曰："室南端，室之正南门。"结句中，"江山"指江水和山脉。

Moonlit Night Feelings from Seeing off Friends in the Riverside Tower（Second of Two Poems with the Same Title）
○By *WANG Bo*
Distinct no more is th' blue stone stair
Veiled in chaotic mist in th' air,
While th' moving high moon shines its light
On th' tower's closed south door at night,
Behind which silent sad farewell
Is bid, and th' river and hills smell
Of dampness and coldness, which make
Them feel their hearts begin to ache.

Annotations to Its Version of English Verse（韵体译诗注释）

1. distinct：*Adjective* readily distinguishable by the senses 可分辨的；明显的 (e.g. a distinct smell of nicotine 可以闻得出尼古丁的味道)

2. th' = the

3. farewell：*Noun* (mass noun) parting good wishes 分别时的美好祝愿 (e.g. He had come on the pretext of bidding her farewell. 他以向她辞行为借口来见她。)

4. smell：*Verb* (no obj.) emit an odour or scent of a specified kind 散发……的气味 (e.g. The place smelled of damp. 这地方散发着潮气。)

第二章 乡情五绝

Chapter 02 About Homesickness

■ 009 ::

静夜思 □李白
床前明月光,疑是地上霜。
举头望明月,低头思故乡。

五绝原诗注释（Annotations to the Original Chinese Version）
　　这是唐代大诗人李白(701—762)的一首五言诗,诗题多种,流行的诗题为《静夜思》,本书从之。首先,有两点需要说明。其一,这首诗的内容存在诸多版本,这里姑且以蘅塘退士的《唐诗三百首》为蓝本,这也几乎是人人耳熟能详的版本,只不过将题目改成目前流行的《静夜思》,而非《夜思》;其二,关于这首诗的"五绝""五古绝"之争。蘅塘退士《唐诗三百首》以及很多选本都将其作为五绝处理,但是也有众多人士提出了质疑。按照五绝的"正律",这首诗的平仄多处不合(还应注意古声中平仄两读的字,以及古平今仄,但却非入声字的字)。但是,如果将诗中多处不合"正律"的地方硬是作为"拗救"来看待的话,李白的这首《静夜思》也就可以算作"五绝"了。鉴于此,再加上"从众心理",这里就将其视作"五绝"。
　　诗人用浅显、直白的语言揭示了内心的乡情之结,寥寥数笔勾勒出一幅月夜里的乡情画面。全诗一气呵成,但上、下句的连接,颇具"蒙太奇"之功,犹如王维的《山中送别》之表现手法。首联"床前明月光,疑是地上霜"写的是诗人在他乡的特定环境中的瞬时感受。这里,对于"床"这样一个意义颇有争议的字,暂且在本书中化复杂为简单,将其视作睡觉之用的"卧榻",也就是现代意义的"床",至于这样的理解与实情是否相符,暂且放置一边。尾联"举头望明月,低头思故乡",颇具现代电影中的"蒙太奇"特色。首联与尾联之间,诗人也许做出了一系列的动作,如披衣下床等,却统统隐去不表。尾联一出,犹如云开雾散,又恰似"虹销雨霁,彩彻区明"(王勃《滕王阁序》)一般。站在月亮之下,抬头仰望,所望之处是"皎皎空中孤月轮"(张若虚《春江花月夜》);一低头,禁不住想起家乡。这种乡情,在如霜明月的映照下,油然而生,毫无遮掩。翘首凝望,俯首沉思——故乡历历在目,亲人如同就在自己的身边。尾联中,一"望",一"思",彼此照应,画面立刻鲜活,栩栩如生。

Random Musing on a Silent Moonlit Night
○By *LI Bai*

Up waking to see pale rays 'head of bed,

As frost on th' ground was I misled.

Outdoors the Moon up there shed light so clear,

Which just made me homesick down here.

N. B. In both ancient and modern China, the moon, be it a bright one or a full one, will always provoke people into various thinking. The full moon in particular always arouses in persons a sense of reunion with their sweetheart, spouse or family.

Annotations to Its Version of English Verse(韵体译诗注释)

1. random: *Adjective* made, done, happening, or chosen without method or conscious decision 胡乱的;无一定规则的;任意的;任意选取的

2. moonlit: *Adjective* lit by the moon 月光照耀下的

3. 'head = ahead

4. th' = the

010 ::

渡汉江 □宋之问

岭外音书断,经冬复历春。

近乡情更怯,不敢问来人。

五绝原诗注释(Annotations to the Original Chinese Version)

关于宋之问(约公元656—712年)这首五言小诗,存在着"作者"之争:一说其作者是初唐时期的宋之问,很多选本将这首诗署上了宋之问的名字,如上海辞书出版社的《唐诗鉴赏辞典》等;一说其作者是中、晚唐时期的李频,如蘅塘退士的《唐诗三百首》中,这首诗的作者就是李频。颇有意思的是,《全唐诗》的第53卷第35首收录的这首诗,署名是宋之问,诗体如上所示;第589卷第55首收录的也是这首诗,署名则变成了李频,不过诗体稍有差别:

岭外音书绝,经年复历春。

近乡情更怯,不敢问来人。

之所以出现这种现象,除了人为的疏忽,记载出错之外,恐怕与宋之问所谓的"人品"有关。尽管如此,人们已经普遍将这首诗视作宋之问的作品了,本书从之,也将其作为宋之问的作品。

欲渡汉江,有所顾忌和忧虑;不渡汉江,心有不甘和牵挂。渡与不渡,那是问题之所在。渡江引发的乡情,这首《渡汉江》给予了微妙而贴切的诠释。

Homesickness Prior to and after Crossing Hanjiang River

○By *SONG Zhi-wen*

In distant south with no message I stay,

With spring coming since winter flies away.

Crossing the river homewards, off I set,

Feeling more upset as I get

Nearer to my birthplace but I dare not

Ask passing villagers a lot.

N. B. The *Hanjiang River* is a river running mostly through today's

Hubei Province, China. It is the location where many historic events took place, hence the popular name mentioned in literature, including poetry. Thus, facing Hanjiang River, people would feel emotional and sentimental.

Annotations to Its Version of English Verse(韵体译诗注释)

1. prior to: before a particular time or event 在……以前;先于;优先于（e.g. She visited me on the day prior to her death. 她去世的前一天还来看我。）

2. message: *Noun* a verbal, written, or recorded communication sent to or left for a recipient who cannot be contacted directly 口信;消息;信息

3. homewards: *Adverb* towards home 向家;朝家;往家

4. sentimental: *Adjective* of or prompted by feelings of tenderness, sadness, or nostalgia 情绪化的;感伤的

011 ::

杂诗　　□王维

君自故乡来,应知故乡事。
来日绮窗前,寒梅著花未?

五绝原诗注释（**Annotations to the Original Chinese Version**）

这首五绝是唐代诗人王维（701—761）的作品,诗题为《杂诗》,一作《杂诗三首（其二）》。其实,王维在这个题目下,一共写了三首诗,算是现代诗里的"组诗"吧。《全唐诗》第128卷第60首收录的就是这组诗,题为《杂诗三首》,上面这首是其中的第二首。跟许多选本一样,这里为方便起见,也将其题目定为《杂诗》,算是化繁就简——虽然有失规范。

王维的这首五绝小诗,在乡情的抒发方面颇具情趣。这种情趣在尾联之中不加修饰地就显露出来了。本来还算是安生的王维,看到故乡的来人,偶然之间,自己的思乡之情就被燃起。看似信手拈来的诗句,看似不经意之间的问话,却在偶然之间,燃起了诗人的乡情——偶发之乡情。尾联中,诗人笔锋一转——看似更加随意的一问,却在无形之中将诗歌的主题做了升华处理:你来的那天,雕刻花

纹的窗户前,那朵顶风冒雪的"寒梅",开花了没有啊?"寒梅"一词,可谓意味深长。

A Poem about an Occasional Homesickness
○By *WANG Wei*
Coming here from our native place,
You should know well its very case.
Before my floral-patterned window,
The day you left, did you behold
Whether the plum blossomed in cold?

N. B. Plum blossom (*Mei* or *Meihua* in Chinese language) is of symbolic meaning in Chinese cultural tradition. It symbolizes endurance, determination, fidelity, elegance, etc. In addition, parents in China are used to naming their daughters after "*Mei*", meaning "plum" or "plum blossom". Besides, a person of female sex usually lives in a house with a *floral-patterned window*—a window carved with floral patterns.

Annotations to Its Version of English Verse(韵体译诗注释)

1. very: *Adjective* (archaic) real, genuine (古旧用法)真正的;真实的

2. case: *Noun* an instance of a particular situation; an example of something occurring 情形;事例;实例

3. floral: *Adjective* decorated with or depicting flowers 饰以花的;描绘花的(e.g. a floral pattern 花卉图案)

4. behold: *Verb* (with obj.) [often in imperative] (archaic or poetic/literary) see or observe (someone or something, especially of remarkable or impressive nature) (古旧用法或诗/文用法)看;观看(尤指看非凡的或感人的人或事物)(e.g. Behold your lord and prince! 看国王和王子!)

5. plum: *Noun* an oval fleshy fruit which is purple, reddish, or yellow when ripe and contains a flattish pointed stone 李子;梅子

6. blossom: *Verb* (no obj.) (of a tree or bush) produce flowers or masses of flowers(树)开花(e.g. a garden in which roses blossom 开着玫瑰花的花园)

7. blossom: *Noun* a flower or a mass of flowers, especially on a tree or bush(尤指树上的)花朵;花簇(e.g. The slopes were ablaze with almond blossom. 山坡上

盛开着扁桃树花。)

8. fidelity：*Noun* (mass noun) faithfulness to a person, cause, or belief, demonstrated by continuing loyalty and support 忠诚；忠实；忠贞

012 ::

滞雨　□李商隐
滞雨长安夜,残灯独客愁。
故乡云水地,归梦不宜秋。

五绝原诗注释（Annotations to the Original Chinese Version）

彼时,诗人李商隐(约813—约858)滞雨长安,雨夜独坐,偏逢瑟瑟秋。于是,心生乡情之结。

尾联"故乡云水地,归梦不宜秋",则笔锋一转,抒发了诗人凝重的情感——乡情之结。当然,这其中也不排除诗人仕途的失意,以及对"夹缝"生存状态的映射。故乡是云水之地,故乡的云,密集蔽日,故乡的水,不断流淌。原来,故乡的雨亦如长安的雨,连绵不断,令归期更加难定。况且,正值天凉好个秋,更是加重了归梦的"不宜"。

A Raining Night in Chang'an

○By *LI Shang-yin*

The autumn rain prolongs the Cap'tal's night,

With one lonely man sitting sad upright

By one single lamp that'll soon cease to light.

The rainy weather in his 'home far'way

And th' wet autumn season in *Chang'an* sway

His dream home at night and during the day.

N. B. *Chang'an*：It is today's Xi'an City, the capital city of Shaanxi Province. As capitals of thirteen dynasties or kingdoms in the long Chinese history, it used to be a holy land for all men of letters. In particular, *Chang'an*, the capital of Tang Dynasty, has become a dream place of poets, who feel it a great honor to go to that place and often mention it in their poetry.

Annotations to Its Version of English Verse（韵体译诗注释）

1. prolong：*Verb*（with obj.）extend the duration of 延长；拖长

2. Cap'tal = Capital

3. 'way = away

4. th' = the

5. sway：*Verb* move or cause to move slowly or rhythmically backwards and forwards or from side to side 摇摆；摆动

6. holy land：*Noun* a place which attracts people of a particular group or with a particular interest 圣地（e.g. Holland is a holy land for jazz enthusiasts. 荷兰是爵士乐狂热者的圣地。）

013 ::

行军九日思长安故园　　□岑参

强欲登高去，无人送酒来。

遥怜故园菊，应傍战场开。

五绝原诗注释（Annotations to the Original Chinese Version）

岑参(约715—770)这首诗的原题后面附了一个括号,内标"时未收长安"。意思是说,当时的长安还在"安史之乱"的叛军手里。诗的题目可谓一篇短短的"序言",交代了诗歌创作的过程、背景、地点以及诗歌的主题——思故园。其实,唐诗中,很多诗题都具有这样的特点。所谓"行军",除了指"军队进行训练或执行任务时从一个地点走到另一个地点"(《现代汉语词典(第五版)》)这一动作性意义外(这往往是现代理解的意义),古代还泛指用兵,如《孙子兵法》的第九篇"行军篇",主要讲述在各种不同地形上处置军队和观察、判断敌情时应该注意的问题。再如,《管子·小问》里面有这样的记载:"桓公曰:'吾已知战胜之器,攻取之数矣,请问行军袭邑,举错而知先后,不失地利,若何?'"另外,"行军"一词在古代还有"行营""军营"之意,岑参的很多诗中所用到的"行军",基本都具有这方面的意义。

欲饮酒,在这个战乱时节,"无人送酒来"——用典却不留痕迹。欲饮酒却"无人送酒来",很是简明、自然。战时登高,当然是"无人送酒来"了。须知,《南史·隐逸列传上》(卷七十五)有一段这样的记载:"尝九月九日无酒,出宅边菊丛中坐久之。逢弘送酒至,即便就酌,醉而后归"。意思是说:有一次过重阳节,陶渊明没有酒喝了,就独自坐在宅边的菊花丛中。坐了很久、很久。不知过了多久,时任江州刺史的王弘送酒来了,陶公这才开怀醉饮,尽兴而归。战乱时期的诗人,不像隐居期间的陶渊明那么幸运,有王弘这样的人送酒来。所以,这首诗首联的对句里,诗人"反向"用典,说"无人送酒来"。艺术效果凸显,引人思考,可谓用笔奇妙,视角奇巧。

Missing My Wartime Home Chang'an at Chongyang Festival
○By *CEN Shen*

Forcing myself to mount the hill subdued,

To bring me wine I find none's in the mood.

Marching afar, I miss my wartime home,

Where I guess poor chrysanthemums abound

Among debris and fumes of th' battle ground.

N. B. *Chang'an* (Today's Xi'an City, Shaanxi Province), the capital city of Tang Dynasty, was then regarded by the poet as his home, for he had been living there for a long time. However, it was then occupied by the rebellious troops, and thus he was forced to march away from it together with the Emperor's troops. One day in the barracks, the poet began to miss his home *Chang'an*, for it was just *Chongyang Festival*, a traditional Chinese festival falling on September 9 of the lunar calendar, when Chinese people usually mount higher places to drink wine and to enjoy the beauty of chrysanthemums, while missing their families.

Annotations to Its Version of English Verse (韵体译诗注释)

1. wartime: *Noun* (mass noun) a period during which a war is taking place (物质名词) 战时

2. mount: *Verb* (with obj.) climb up (stairs, a hill, or other rising surface) 登(楼梯、山或其他上升面)

3. subdued: *Adjective* (of a person or their manner) quiet and rather reflective

or depressed(人或举止)抑制的;克制的;低沉的;抑郁的

4. be in the mood for sth./doing sth.; be in the mood to do sth.: to have a strong desire to do sth.; feel like doing sth. 有心情做某事;想(或有意)做某事

5. afar: *Adverb* (chiefly poetic literary) at or to a distance(主要用在诗性文学中)在远方;向远方(e.g. Our hero travelled afar. 我们的英雄一路远行。)

6. abound: *Verb* (no obj.) exist in large numbers or amounts 大量存在

7. debris: *Noun* (mass noun) scattered pieces of rubbish or remains 碎片;残骸

8. fume: *Noun* (usu. fumes) gas, smoke, or vapour that smells strongly or is dangerous to inhale 刺鼻(或有害)的气;烟;汽

9. barracks: *Plural Noun* (often treated as sing.) a large building or group of buildings used to house soldiers 兵营;营房

10. th' = the

014 ::

关山月二首(其一)　□戴叔伦

月出照关山,秋风人未还。
清光无远近,乡泪半书间。

五绝原诗注释(Annotations to the Original Chinese Version)

戴叔伦(732—789)以"关山月"为题的五绝共有两首,这是其中的第一首。此诗寓情于景,写出了雄伟和苍凉,衬托出诗人的人生境遇及思乡情结。诗题中,"关山月"属于"乐府诗题,《乐府诗集》列入《横吹曲辞》,引《乐府解题》曰:'《关山月》,伤别离也。'"①由此可见,"关山月"属乐府旧题中的"横吹曲辞"之列,多抒发离别之情和哀伤之感。其中的"关山"(包括首句中的"关山"),一种可能是关隘和山峦或险关和高山的合称,一种可能是指位于甘肃省天水市的一座山脉,古时候称作"陇山",是历史上出了名的难以翻越的山,古人至此,多有哀叹。也就是说,这里的"关山"可能是泛指,也可能是专指,本书著者认为其泛指的可能性较大。

---

① 转引自"霍松林,1991:312"。

此诗首联不入对,但首句入韵。首联对句中的"人"指"征戍之人"(霍松林,1991:427)。戍边逢秋,月照边关,难免起意,思念故园。尾联中,"清光"意为清亮的光,诗中指月光;"半书间"或者意为家书读到一半的时候,或者意为家书写到一半的时候。另外,"半书间",一作"半宵间"。

Sentimental Feelings upon Seeing the Moon over the Mountain Pass(First of Two Poems with the Same Title)

○By *DAI Shu-lun*

English Verse(1)

O'er th' mountain pass the rising moon

Shines brightly far and near,

While cold autumnal wind blows soon,

But he's still on th' frontier,

One letter from his home in hands,

Two streams of tears from glands.

English Verse(2)

O'er th' mountain pass the rising moon

Shines brightly far and near,

While cold autumnal wind blows soon,

But he's still on th' frontier—

A letter to home writt'n half way,

He's crying like a stray.

N. B. In both ancient and modern China, the moon, be it a bright one or a full one, will always provoke people into various thinking. The full moon in particular always arouses in persons a sense of reunion with their sweetheart, spouse or family.

Annotations to Its Version of English Verse(韵体译诗注释)

1. sentimental: *Adjective* of or prompted by feelings of tenderness, sadness, or nostalgia 情绪化的;感伤的 (e.g. She felt a sentimental attachment to the place creep over her. 她感到一种对该地的依恋感遍布她的全身。)

2. pass：*Noun* a route over or through mountains（山坳）通道；山口（e.g. The pass over the mountain was open again after the snows. 过山的通道在下雪后又重新开放了。)

3. verse：*Noun*（mass noun）writing arranged with a metrical rhythm, typically having a rhyme 诗；韵文；诗句

4. O'er = Over

5. th' = the

6. far and near：everywhere 到处；处处；四面八方（e.g. People came from far and near to the party. 人们从各处来参加聚会。）

7. autumnal：*Adjective* of, characteristic of, or occurring in autumn 秋季的；秋季出现（或发生）的（e.g. rich autumnal colours 绚丽多彩的秋色）

8. frontier：*Noun* a line or border separating two countries 边境；边界

9. gland：*Noun* an organ in the human or animal body which secretes particular chemical substances for use in the body or for discharge into the surroundings（人或动物体内的）腺

10. writt'n = written

11. stray：*Noun* a lost or homeless person, esp. a child 迷路的人或无家可归的人(特别是孩子)

■ **015** ::

西过渭州见渭水思秦川　　□岑参

渭水东流去，何时到雍州。

凭添两行泪，寄向故园流。

五绝原诗注释（Annotations to the Original Chinese Version）

岑参(约715—770)原籍南阳(今河南新野)，后迁居江陵。所以，岑参当属江陵(今湖北江陵)人。但是，由于诗人有一大部分时间生活在当时的都城长安，长安也就成了诗人的第二故乡。正因如此，岑参诗中的乡情之结有不少体现在故园长安上面，如《西过渭州见渭水思秦川》。当时，诗人西行经过渭州，看见向东流淌的渭水，就思念起自己的故乡长安，于是有感而发遂成此诗。诗题中的"渭州"，位于今甘肃省陇西县西南，渭州的鸟鼠山是渭水的发源地。渭水向东流

至陕西境内,在陕西境内流入黄河。诗题中的"秦川","即关中,唐长安城所在地"(霍松林,1991:157),所以诗人岑参在诗中就以秦川指代自己的家乡了。同样,诗人在首联对句中借"雍州"指代自己的家乡长安,因长安所在地正是雍州,据《旧唐书·地理志》记载,"京兆府……武德元年改为雍州……开元元年,改雍州为京兆府。"①

诗人在此诗中采用了一种类似拟人的修辞手法,首联中诗人问渭水什么时候能流到雍州,也就是诗人岑参的家乡长安,为尾联的思乡情结做铺设。尾联中,"凭"有请求之意,整联的意思大致是说:请将我的两行思乡的热泪添加到渭水中,让我的泪水随着渭水快快流向故园长安吧。

The Sight of Weishui River Makes Me Think of Chang'an, My Hometown in Qinchuan or Yongzhou, While Traveling West through Weizhou

○By *CEN Shen*

"When will you, th' Weishui River, flow
East to Chang'an, where up I grow?"
Ask I. "Please add two streams of my
Homesick tears to your course," I cry,
"And lead them as fast as you can
To th' home I oft dream of, Chang'an."

N. B. Weishui River (Today's Weihe River) in ancient China, which rises in the mountains of ancient China's Weizhou region and flows east before entering the Yellow River in today's Shaanxi Province, thus forming its largest tributary, flows through ancient China's Chang'an City (Today's Xi'an City, Shaanxi Province), the capital of Tang Dynasty and the hometown of CEN Shen, the poet of the above poem. Located in area

---

① 转引自"霍松林,1991:157"。

of Qinchuan, Chang'an was once under the administrative jurisdiction of Yongzhou, and hence in this poem, the poet respectively substitutes Qinchuan and Yongzhou for his hometown, Chang'an.

Annotations to Its Version of English Verse(韵体译诗注释)

1. th' = the

2. homesick：*Adjective* experiencing a longing for one's home during a period of absence from it 想家的；思乡的

3. course：*Noun* (in sing.) the route or direction followed by a ship, aircraft, road, or river (船、飞机、路或河流的)所经之路；路线

4. oft = often

5. tributary：*Noun* a river or stream flowing into a larger river or lake (河川或湖泊的)支流

6. jurisdiction：*Noun* (mass noun) the official power to make legal decisions and judgements 司法权；裁判权

7. substitute：*Verb* (with obj.) use or add in place of 用……代替 (e.g. Dried rosemary can be substituted for the fresh herb. 干迷迭香可用来代替鲜草。)

016 ::

绝句二首(其二)　□杜甫
江碧鸟逾白，山青花欲燃。
今春看又过，何日是归年。

五绝原诗注释(Annotations to the Original Chinese Version)

唐代伟大的现实主义诗人杜甫(712—770)被后世尊为"诗圣"，与李白并称"李杜"。杜甫的《绝句二首》由两首五绝组成，此诗为其中的第二首，为诗人杜甫入蜀后所作，抒发了诗人客居他乡时心生乡情的感叹。

此诗首联入对，但首句不入韵。首联以景起兴，具有强烈的色彩对比，画面感极强。尾联则表达了诗人漂泊异乡之际对家乡的思念之情，即诗人的乡愁情结。整首诗可以说是以乐景衬托哀情。首句中，"鸟"指江上的鸥鸟，"逾"为更加之意。

Two Quatrains with Five Chinese Characters to Each Line (Second of Two Poems with the Same Title)

○By *DU Fu*

Above green river water fly

Gulls white, whiter than they're in th' sky,

While on green mounts the flowers red

Appear to burn like th' sun instead.

This spring's about to fade away,

But when will be th' home-going day?

Annotations to Its Version of English Verse（韵体译诗注释）

1. quatrain: *Noun* a stanza of four lines, especially one having alternate rhymes（尤指隔行押韵的）四行诗节；四行诗

2. gull: *Noun* a long-winged web-footed seabird with a raucous call, typically having white plumage with a grey or black mantle 鸥

3. th' = the

4. mount: *Noun* a mountain or hill (archaic except in place names)（除用于地名外均为古义）山；丘

第三章 友情五绝

Chapter 03 About Friendship

■ **017** ::

秋夜寄丘员外 □韦应物
怀君属秋夜，散步咏凉天。
山空松子落，幽人应未眠。

五绝原诗注释（Annotations to the Original Chinese Version）

这是唐代诗人韦应物(737—约792)的一首五言诗，诗题为《秋夜寄丘员外》，其中的"丘员外"，有的版本亦为"邱员外"。另外，《全唐诗》第188卷第55首载有此诗，标题为《秋夜寄丘二十二员外》。不管怎样，韦应物这首诗里所怀之人指的是当时正在临平山学道的丘丹或邱丹。他是苏州人，曾拜为尚书郎，后隐居临平山上。由于其在家族中排行第二十二位，亦称其为"丘二十二员外"或"邱二十二员外"。

这首五言诗不符"正律"，且联间"失黏"，实属"五古绝"，但很多选本仍将之做"五绝"处理，如蘅塘退士的《唐诗三百首》等。还有名家将这首诗视作诗人韦应物的五绝代表作之一。故本书从之，也将其视作"五绝"加以研究与翻译。首句中"君"和结句中的"幽人"都是指诗人的朋友——丘员外，即丘丹。

An Autumn Night Poem to My Friend QIU Dan, an Extra Vice-minister

○By *WEI Ying-wu*

I miss my friend just on this autumn night,
While walking under the sky cold.
Falling on still hill ground are pine nuts light,
And he'd not sleep with thoughts untold.

Annotations to Its Version of English Verse(韵体译诗注释)

1. extra：*Adjective* added to an existing or usual amount or number 额外的；分外的；外加的

2. untold：*Adjective* (of a story or event) not narrated or recounted(故事或事件)未说过的；未被讲述的

018 ::

相思　□王维

红豆生南国，秋来发几枝？
愿君多采撷，此物最相思。

五绝原诗注释（Annotations to the Original Chinese Version）

这首诗中，诗人王维(701—761)抒发的是对友人深深的情谊，实为友情五绝中的典范之作。诗人借红豆寄托对友人的思念，抒发了诗人赤诚的友情。

关于这首诗有两点需要说明一下：一是这首诗的异文性，二是这首诗所抒发的情感问题。关于这首诗的异文性，这首诗有许多不同的版本，某些地方的用字各不相同。例如，有"愿君多采撷"和"劝君多采撷"之分；有"劝君多采撷"和"劝君休采撷"之分；有"春来发几枝"和"秋来发几枝"之分；有"红豆生南国"和"红杏生南国"之分；有"秋来发几枝"和"秋来发故枝"之分；还有"愿君多采撷"和"赠君多采撷"之分，等等。关于这首诗所抒发的情感问题，主要有两类看法：一类看法认为这是首爱情诗，抒发了两情相悦之思；另一类看法认为这是一首思念友人之诗，抒发的是对友人的怀念之情，本书从后者。

Red Berries

○ By *WANG Wei*

The tree with berries red grows on south lands;
How many reds adorn the autumn view?
Wish that to th' full you'd pluck them with your hands,
For they best show a friend's thinking of you.

Annotations to Its Version of English Verse(韵体译诗注释)

1. berry: *Noun* a small roundish juicy fruit without a stone 无核浆果
2. red: *Noun* a red thing or person, in particular (尤指)红色物(或人)
3. adorn: *Verb* [with obj.] make more beautiful or attractive 装饰 (e.g. Pictures and prints adorned his walls. 画和复制画装饰着他的墙面。)
4. view: *Count. Noun* a sight or prospect, typically of attractive natural scenery, that can be taken in by the eye from a particular place 景色;美景 (e. g. a fine view of the castle 城堡的美景)
5. th' = the
6. to the full: to the greatest possible extent 彻底地;充分地
7. pluck: *Verb* (with obj.) take hold of (something) and quickly remove it from its place 摘;采;拔;取

019 ::

问刘十九　　□白居易

绿蚁新醅酒,红泥小火炉。
晚来天欲雪,能饮一杯无?

五绝原诗注释（Annotations to the Original Chinese Version）

白居易(772—846)的这首五绝,首联入对,以强烈的对比烘托出一幅温馨画面——绿蚁新醅酒,红泥小火炉:家中新酿的米酒可以喝了,只不过没有过滤(醅[pēi],意为没滤过的酒),表面上泛起了一层"绿蚁"——颜色微绿、形细如蚁的酒渣,但芳香四溢,香气扑鼻,而且红泥做的小火炉烧起来了,旺旺的,屋子里已经是暖意融融。

在《问刘十九》这首诗中,诗人在即将飘雪的寒夜,邀请朋友前来对饮,表达了对朋友暖暖的情意。据史料记载,白居易一生中结交了很多朋友,从其诗歌之中可以体会出他对友情的珍重。真可谓:真诚一问,友情凸显。欲雪之夜虽寒,对酌之意尤暖。此乃寒夜友情是也。

A Question to LIU Shi-jiu, a Friend of Mine
○By *BAI Ju-yi*
"Green ants" o'er newly brewed rice wine abound,
While red clay stove burns bright above the ground.
With even being darker, it looks like snow—
"Would you come over for some drinks, my bro?"

N. B. In the first line, "green ants" refer to a layer of green substance, which looks like green ants floating on the surface of unskimmed newly-fermented rice wine, making it look so inviting and tasty.

Annotations to Its Version of English Verse(韵体译诗注释)

1. o'er = over

2. abound:*Verb*(no obj.)exist in large numbers or amounts 大量存在

3. even:*Noun*(archaic or poetic/literary)(古旧用法或诗/文用法)the end of the day; evening 黄昏;傍晚(e. g. Bring it to my house this even. 今晚把它带到我家里来。)

4. bro:*Noun*(informal)short for brother(非正式用法)brother 的简称

020 ::

留卢秦卿　□司空曙
知有前期在,难分此夜中。
无将故人酒,不及石尤风。

五绝原诗注释(Annotations to the Original Chinese Version)
这首在临别时分表达浓浓朋友之情的五绝《留卢秦卿》,为唐代诗人司空曙(约720—约790~794)所作(一作《郎士元诗》),是送别诗,更是散发出友情芬芳的诗。关于诗题,有的版本亦作《送卢秦卿》(俞陛云,2011:135),不知何故。但是,本书著者感觉还是《留卢秦卿》较为达意,这也应该是原始版本的诗题吧。

尾联中，诗人笔锋一转，将临别友情推向了极致："无将故人酒，不及石尤风。"不要使老朋友的酒，抵不上那阻客而行的石尤风啊。换言之，一定得让老朋友这临行的酒，抵得上那阻客而行的石尤风。这收尾之笔，看似平淡，实则铿锵有力，借"故人酒"一番发挥，引出"石尤风"。"石尤风"者，古代主要有两种解释：

一种是从传说角度解释的，元代伊世珍辑《琅嬛记》引《江湖纪闻》曰："石尤风者，传闻为石氏女，嫁为尤郎妇，情好甚笃，为商远行，妻阻之，不从。尤出不归，妻忆之病亡，临亡长叹曰：'吾恨不能阻其行，以至于此。今凡有商旅远行，吾当作大风，为天下妇人阻之。'自后商旅发船，值打头逆风，则曰：'此石尤风也。'遂止不行。妇人以夫姓为名，故曰'石尤'。"①

另一种解释见于明代周婴《卮林补遗·石尤》："《杨用修外集》：'石尤，江中水虫名，此虫出必有恶风，舟人目打头风曰石尤，犹岭南人曰飓母，黄河人曰孟婆也。'用修此解似得之，但亦未见所出，且以为水虫太么麼矣。"②

其中，第二种解释未免有牵强附会之感，但不失为一种说法。这两种说法都将"石尤风"诠释为"逆风、顶头风、打头风"，这在唐诗句中也屡见不鲜。

Stay, LU Qin-qing, My Old Friend
○By *SIKONG Shu*

Knowing a chance to meet never fails,
Tonight I'm still sad to part with you.
Before your boat leaves, I hope in lieu
Of fierce adverse winds blocking your sails,
This very last cup of farewell wine will be
A hindrance to your leaving from me.

---

① 伊世珍辑《琅嬛记》卷中，《四库全书存目丛书》本，转引自"白建忠，2013(4)：151"。

② 周婴《卮林》，《丛书集成初编》本，转引自"白建忠，2013(4)：151"。

Annotations to Its Version of English Verse(韵体译诗注释)

1. lieu: *Noun* (in phrase in lieu) instead 替代(e. g. The company issued additional shares to shareholders in lieu of a cash dividend. 这家公司给股票持有者送股,而不是现金分红。)

2. adverse: *Adjective* preventing success or development; harmful; unfavourable 阻碍成功(或发展)的;有害的;不利的(e. g. adverse weather conditions 不利的天气条件)

3. hindrance: *Noun* a thing that provides resistance, delay, or obstruction to something or someone 阻碍(物);妨碍

021 ::

答陆澧 □张九龄
松叶堪为酒,春来酿几多。
不辞山路远,踏雪也相过。

五绝原诗注释(Annotations to the Original Chinese Version)
《全唐诗》第49卷第62首为《答陆澧》,作者是张九龄(678—740),但颇为有趣、无独有偶的是第315卷第13首诗题也是《答陆澧》,作者却变成了朱放。因此,这首诗的原作者是谁,存在着争议。尽管如此,鉴于目前流行的提法以张九龄为主,本书从之,将《答陆澧》视为张九龄的作品。张九龄《答陆澧》中的"陆澧",应为张九龄的友人,但其生平不详。

整首五绝短短二十个字,虽字字质朴,但却可以说字字珠玑。亲切、自然、流畅的语言,道出的是朋友间那言之不尽的情谊。质朴的语言道出质朴的情谊,友情深厚,却没有借助深厚的语言来传达,唯借助质朴之语寄质朴之深情。

Reply to My Friend LU Li's Invitation to a Gathering
○By *ZHANG Jiu-ling*
Since wine be made with needles of pine,
In this spring how much've you done such wine?

Then, 'ven far, far away, your home'll be
Reach'd by taking mountain road bumpy,
And were it cover'd with heavy snow,
I'll go drink to my heart's content, though.

Annotations to Its Version of English Verse(韵体译诗注释)

1. gathering: *Noun* an assembly or meeting, especially a social or festive one or one held for a specific purpose(尤指为社交、过节或特定目的举办的)聚会;集会

2. much've = much have

3. 'ven = even

4. Reach'd = Reached

5. bumpy: *Adjective* (bumpier, bumpiest) (of a surface) uneven, with many patches raised above the rest 颠簸的;崎岖不平的

6. cover'd = covered

7. to one's heart's content: to the full extent of one's desires 心满意足地;尽情地(e.g. The children could run and play to their heart's content. 孩子们能尽情地奔跑玩耍。)

■ 022 ::

逢谢偃 □高适
红颜怆为别,白发始相逢。
唯馀昔时泪,无复旧时容。

五绝原诗注释(Annotations to the Original Chinese Version)

虽谢偃为何人已无法考证,但从《逢谢偃》一诗中可以断定其为诗人高适(约700~704—765)的一位老朋友,情谊深厚。年轻的时候彼此分别,悲伤不已(原诗中的"怆"[chuàng],悲伤之意),再次相见彼此都已白发苍苍。老朋友相见,昔日的泪水依旧(原诗中的"馀"[yú],同"余"),言情谊如初。可是,沧海桑田,昔日的容貌都不复从前了。此诗两联皆人对,以强烈的反差凸显友情之珍贵。其中,首联基本上属于工对,首句不入韵;尾联则属宽对。可谓:光阴荏苒,时不我待。情谊依旧,面容已改。

Seeing Once Again XIE Yan, My Old Friend
○By *GAO Shi*

When young we sadly bid goodbye,

And ever since then ages flew;

Today I once again see you,

Our grey hair not hard to descry.

Unchanged remain tears of us two,

And gone are our young faces though.

Annotations to Its Version of English Verse（韵体译诗注释）

1. bid：*Verb* (bidding; past bid or bade; past participle bid) (with obj.) utter (a greeting or farewell) to 向……表示问候；向……告别（e.g. a chance to bid farewell to their president and welcome the new man 告别旧总裁、欢迎新总裁的难得机会）

2. descry：*Verb* to discover by careful observation or scrutiny; detect 看出；辨认出

023 ::

林塘怀友　□王勃

芳屏画春草,仙杼织朝霞。

何如山水路,对面即飞花。

五绝原诗注释（Annotations to the Original Chinese Version）

在《林塘怀友》这首五绝中,王勃(约650—约676)以别致的手法表达了对友人的思念。这种手法婉转、含蓄,并非直截了当、直抒胸臆。这种友情的抒发,诗题具有一定的提示作用。诗题中,"林塘"为树林和池塘的合称,多用于指代幽居之所。与友人分别后,幽居之所的"芳屏"(美丽漂亮的屏风)上画着的"春草春花如同仙女的机杼织出的云锦般美丽"（霍松林,1991:42）。尽管如此,这一切"何如"(怎么能比得上)两旁有山有水的道路,风中飞舞的鲜花随处可见。屏风上春花春草虽芳,莫如在大自然中接触到真草真花,实则表达了对友人的思念,渴望与友人见面叙谈。

Thinking of My Friend from Where I Live in Seclusion
○By *WANG Bo*

So fair on th' screen are th' springtime bloom
And grass as to look like th' brocade
Of morn clouds wove by th' fairy maid
With th' help of her attractive loom.
However fair they are, how can
They be far more beautiful than
The dancing flowers before me
While walking on the road, each side
Of which is decked with mounts and wide
Waters, like seeing friends in glee!

Annotations to Its Version of English Verse(韵体译诗注释)

1. seclusion: *Noun* (mass noun) the state of being private and away from other people 隔绝;隐居(e.g. They enjoyed ten days of peace and seclusion. 他们享受了十天与世隔绝的宁静生活。)

2. fair: *Adjective* (archaic) beautiful; attractive(古旧用法)美丽的;动人的;有魅力的(e.g. the fairest of her daughters 她女儿中最漂亮的一位)

3. th' = the

4. bloom: *Noun* a flower, especially one cultivated for its beauty(尤指供观赏的)花

5. brocade: *Noun* (mass noun) a rich fabric, usually silk, woven with a raised pattern, typically with gold or silver thread(尤指用金银线)织出凸花纹(或图案的)织锦锦缎

6. morn: *Noun* poetic/literary term for morning(诗/文用法)同"morning"

7. weave: *Verb* (past wove; past participle woven or wove) (no obj.) (usu. as noun weaving) make fabric in this way, typically by working at a loom(尤指用织布机)纺织;织布

8. loom: *Noun* an apparatus for making fabric by weaving yarn or thread 织机

9. deck: *Verb* (with obj.) (usu. be decked) decorate or adorn brightly or festively 装饰;打扮

10. mount: *Noun* a mountain or hill (archaic except in place names)(除用于地名外均为古义)山；丘

11. glee: *Noun* (mass noun) great delight(物质名词)欢快；欣喜

024 ::

送朱大入秦　　□孟浩然
游人武陵去,宝剑直千金。
分手脱相赠,平生一片心。

五绝原诗注释(Annotations to the Original Chinese Version)

在《送朱大入秦》诗题中提到的"朱大"应是诗人孟浩然(689—740)的友人"朱去非"(霍松林,1991：225),因其在家族兄弟中排行老大,故人称"朱大";诗题中以"秦"指代唐代都城长安(今陕西省西安市)。另外,首句提到的"五陵"也用来指代长安,因汉代五个帝王的陵墓(汉高祖长陵、惠帝安陵、景帝阳陵、武帝茂陵、昭帝平陵)基本上都设在长安,并实行陵邑制,影响深远。首联出句中的"游人"本指游客,诗中借指朱大;首联对句中的"直",一作"值","直千金"言宝剑之名贵。

Parting with ZHU Da, My Dear Friend Who Leaves for Chang'an in Qin Region

○By *MENG Hao-ran*

My friend to Chang'an travels, where

Lies Wuling, th' Five-tomb Zone well-known,

Wearing his sword priceless and rare,

For 'tis presented to him 'lone

At the time when with him I part

To show some feelings in my heart.

N. B. Chang'an: It is today's Xi'an City, the capital city of Shaanxi Province. Wuling, or Five-tomb Zone (or Five-tomb Region), is a large area in Chang'an, which lies in the region of Qin. In Wuling, there are five tombs of Han Dynasty's emperors, and so it ("Wuling"), along with "Qin" or the "region of Qin", is often used in literary works to replace Chang'an. As capitals of thirteen dynasties or kingdoms in the long Chinese history, Chang'an used to be a holy land for all men of letters. In particular, as the capital of Tang Dynasty, it has become a dream place of poets, who feel it a great honor to go to that place and often mention it in their poetry.

Annotations to Its Version of English Verse(韵体译诗注释)

1. th' = the

2. priceless: *Adjective* so precious that its value cannot be determined 贵重的；无价的；无法估价的；稀世之珍的（e.g. priceless works of art 艺术珍品）

3. 'tis = it is

4. 'lone = alone: *Adverb* indicating that something is confined to the specified subject or recipient 只仅仅（e.g. It was a smile for him alone. 那是一个只给他一人的微笑。）

5. holy land: *Noun* (as noun a holy land) a place which attracts people of a particular group or with a particular interest 圣地（e.g. Holland is a holy land for jazz enthusiasts. 荷兰是爵士乐狂热者的圣地。）

第四章 闲适五绝

Chapter 04 About Unrestrainedness

025 ::

江雪 □柳宗元

千山鸟飞绝,万径人踪灭。

孤舟蓑笠翁,独钓寒江雪。

五绝原诗注释(Annotations to the Original Chinese Version)

柳宗元(773—819)的这首五言四行仄韵诗,跟前述的某些诗一样,如李白的《静夜思》等,存在着诗的体式之疑,即"五绝""五古绝"之疑。蘅塘退士的《唐诗三百首》等将其列为"五言绝句"之列,即"五绝",本书从之,将其视作"五绝"。

这首诗用仄韵,但非纯粹的仄声韵,准确说是"入声韵"。对于仄韵诗,向来说法不一,包括其是否应为格律诗之争。还有人认为用仄韵难以写出神韵,因仄声字(包括入声字)容易让人产生压抑的心理反应,不利于诗境的铺陈。但是,柳宗元的这首诗用的是仄韵,却取得了理想的效果:意境清冷,却并不令人产生多少压抑的心理反应,雪中的闲适之情也就跃然纸上了。

An Angler in Snow

○By *LIU Zong-yuan*

'Mong mountains birds no more be found;

'Long lines of path footprints are drown'd.

One lonely boat bears one man old

With straw cape and bamboo hat cold

Angling alone o'er one river

Encircled by snow, with no shiver.

Annotations to Its Version of English Verse（韵体译诗注释）

1. angler: *Noun* a person who fishes with a rod and line 钓鱼人；垂钓者

2. 'Mong = Among

3. 'Long = Along

4. drown'd = drowned

5. bear: *Verb* (of a vehicle or boat) convey (passengers or cargo)（车或船）运输；运送 (e. g. Steamboats bear the traveller out of Kerrerra Sound. 汽船把游客送出凯勒拉海峡。)

6. cape: *Noun* a sleeveless cloak, typically a short one(尤指短)无袖斗篷

7. bamboo: *Noun* (mass noun) a giant woody grass which grows chiefly in the tropics, where it is widely cultivated 竹；竹子

8. angle: *Verb* (no obj.) fish with a rod and line 钓鱼；垂钓

9. o'er = over

10. shiver: *Noun* a momentary trembling movement 颤抖；发抖(e. g. She gave a little shiver as the wind flicked at her bare arms. 当风拂过她裸露的手臂时,她颤抖了一下。)

■ 026 ::

寻隐者不遇　　□贾岛

松下问童子,言师采药去。

只在此山中,云深不知处。

五绝原诗注释（**Annotations to the Original Chinese Version**）

关于这首小诗,存在着"作者"之争：诗题不同,作者不同,但诗体

完全相同。一说其作者是诗僧贾岛(779—843),诗题为《寻隐者不遇》,很多选本将这首诗署上了贾岛的名字,如李淼(2007)注释的《唐诗三百首》等;一说其作者是宪宗朝官监察御史孙革,诗题为《访羊尊师》,如刘永济(1981)选释的《唐人绝句精华》中,这首诗的作者就是孙革。对于这一"烫手的山芋",有些选本干脆做了兼顾处理:说作者是贾岛时,诗题写作《寻隐者不遇(一作孙革访羊尊师诗)》;说作者是孙革时,诗题写作《访羊尊师(一作贾岛诗)》,或做类似的处理。颇有意思的是,《全唐诗》第473卷第24首收录的是这首诗,署名是孙革,而第574卷第100首收录的也是这首诗,署名则变成了贾岛。不管实情如何,本书将这首诗的作者定位到贾岛身上,即贾岛所作《寻隐者不遇》。

A Visit of the Recluse Only to Find HE Is Absent
○By *JIA Dao*

Beneath a pine 'bout HIM I ask the boy,

Who says HE is away to gather herbs.

"HE's just on this mountain," he adds with joy,

"But on finding HIS tracks dense clouds form curbs."

Annotations to Its Version of English Verse(韵体译诗注释)

1. recluse: *Noun* a person who lives a solitary life and tends to avoid other people 隐士;遁世者

2. absent: *Adjective* not present in a place or at an occasion 不在(场)的;缺席的

3. beneath: *Preposition* extending directly underneath, typically with close contact(尤指紧挨)在……下方

4. pine: *Noun* (also pine tree) an evergreen coniferous tree which has clusters of long needle-shaped leaves. Many kinds are grown for the soft timber, which is widely used for furniture and pulp, or for tar and turpentine 松树

5. 'bout = about

6. herb: *Noun* any plant with leaves, seeds, or flowers used for flavouring, food, medicine, or perfume 芳草植物;药用植物

7. track: *Noun* (usu. tracks) a mark or line of marks left by a person, animal,

or vehicle in passing 足迹；踪迹；车辙（e. g. He followed the tracks made by the police cars in the snow. 他跟随着警车在雪上留下的痕迹。）

8. form：*Verb* go to make up or constitute 构成；组成（e. g. the precepts which form the basis of the book 构成本书基础的规则）

9. curb：*Noun* a check or restraint on something 控制；约束；抑制（e. g. plans to introduce tougher curbs on insider dealing 对内部交易引入更严格控制的方案）

027 ::

春晓　□孟浩然
春眠不觉晓，处处闻啼鸟。
夜来风雨声，花落知多少。

五绝原诗注释（Annotations to the Original Chinese Version）
孟浩然（689—740）所作的这首《春晓》，诗题不止这一个。根据李景白（1988）和徐鹏（1989）等人的校注，此诗宋本题作《春晚绝句》，而《唐百家诗》则题作《春晚》。若排除联间失黏这一因素（一说仄韵诗联间允许失黏）及仄韵诗是否为格律诗之争，这也是一首五言绝句，押仄韵，为唐代诗人孟浩然所作。尾联出句"夜来风雨声"，一作"欲知昨夜风"；尾联对句"花落知多少"，一作"花落无多少"。

孟浩然的一首《春晓》，平淡无奇，却家喻户晓，千古传唱。诗人从春天的一个平常之举——"春眠"着笔，一路铺陈，顺畅自然地引出诗人的情感——"花落知多少"，喜春、惜春、伤春之情掺杂，溢于言表。

At Dawn of a Spring Day
○By *MENG Hao-ran*
While dreams last longer than day-break,
Birds twitter all 'round for th' sun's sake.
How many flowers fall in pain
Because of last night's wind and rain?

Annotations to Its Version of English Verse（韵体译诗注释）
1. dawn：*Noun* the first appearance of light in the sky before sunrise 黎明；拂

晓;晨曦(e. g. He set off at dawn. 他黎明时分出发。)

2. daybreak：*Noun* the time in the morning when daylight first appears；dawn 黎明;破晓

3. twitter：*Verb*（no obj.）（of a bird）give a call consisting of repeated light tremulous sounds(鸟)吱吱叫;啁啾

4. 'round ＝ around

5. th' ＝ the

6. sake：*Noun*（for the sake of something or for something's sake）for the purpose of；in the interest of；in order to achieve or preserve 为了……目的;为了……的利益;为了（e. g. The couple moved to the coast for the sake of her health. 那对夫妇为了她的健康搬到沿海地区居住。）

7. because of：on account of；by reason of；owing to；由于;因为

This phrase typically precedes the reason that something else has happened. 本短语典型的用法,就是位于引起另一件事情发生的原因前。

（e. g. I just found out that the event has been canceled because of the snow. 我刚刚得知,由于下雪,赛事取消了。）

028 ::

登鹳雀楼　　□王之涣

白日依山尽,黄河入海流。

欲穷千里目,更上一层楼。

五绝原诗注释（Annotations to the Original Chinese Version）

这首《登鹳雀楼》也存在着作者之疑,《全唐诗》第253卷第1首诗题是这样写的:"登鹳雀楼(一作朱斌诗)",也就是说,有人把这首诗当成朱斌的作品。此外,还有人认为此诗为朱佐日所作。但是,这样的作者之疑,可以"拨乱反正",这与本书中提到的《渡汉江》《寻隐者不遇》性质上不太一样。李裕民经过一番论证,认为"此诗真正作者乃一介布衣朱斌,原诗名为《登楼》。自《文苑英华》后诸名家大作多从王之涣说,朱斌之名几湮灭不闻。如今真相大白,应当还《登鹳雀楼》本来面目,以使原作者诗史留名,尊重其著作权"(李裕民,2015[1]：67)。也许是宋代李昉、徐铉等人在编撰《文苑英华》时犯的错误,将此诗署为王之涣(688—742),广泛流传至今。本书只好"将错就错",采取流行的说法,视《登鹳雀楼》为王之涣的作品。

此诗以短短二十个字写出了游览中的闲适,但闲适中见壮阔,闲适中透真知。在创作手法上,诗人在并不要求对仗的绝句中采用了对仗的手法,且不"对"则已,一"对"成"双":全诗共两联,两联皆对仗。首联属工对,尾联属流水对。虽如此,却并不显得呆板、僵化,而是自然流畅,毫无人工雕琢之痕,难怪沈德潜在《唐诗别裁》中对这首诗做了高度评价:"四语皆对,读来不嫌其排,骨高故也。"

Upon Mounting the Stork Tower

○By *WANG Zhi-huan*

The scorching sun behind ranges descends,
While th' Yellow River is surging seaward.
In case one more set of steps one ascends,
There will be further view to be captured.

Annotations to Its Version of English Verse(韵体译诗注释)

1. upon: *Preposition* on the occasion of, at the time of, or immediately after 在……时;紧接着……(e. g. She was joyful upon seeing her child take his first steps. 看到自己的孩子开始迈步走路,她很开心。)

2. mount: *Verb* (with obj.) climb up (stairs, a hill, or other rising surface) 登 (楼梯、山或其他上升面)

3. stork: *Noun* a very tall long-legged wading bird with a long heavy bill and typically with white and black plumage 鹳

4. scorching: *Adjective* very hot 炎热的

5. range: *Noun* a line or series of mountains or hills 山脉

6. descend: *Verb* to move from a higher to a lower place; come or go down 下降;下落

7. th' = the

8. surge: *Verb* (no obj., usu. with adverbial) (of a crowd or a natural force) move suddenly and powerfully forward or upward(人群或自然力)汹涌;奔腾(e. g. The journalists surged forward. 记者们蜂拥向前。)

9. seaward: *Adverb* (also seawards) towards the sea 朝海;面向海(e. g. After

about a mile they turned seaward. 约一海里之后,他们调头驶向大海。)

10. in case:If it happens that; if 倘若;如果(e.g. The meeting will be put off in case it should rain. 倘若下雨,会议延期举行。)

11. ascend:Verb (with obj.) go up or climb 登上;攀登(e.g. She ascended the stairs. 她上了楼。)

12. further:Adjective (also farther) more distant in space than another item of the same kind(距离上)更远的;较远的

029 ::

答人　□太上隐者
偶来松树下,高枕石头眠。
山中无历日,寒尽不知年。

五绝原诗注释(Annotations to the Original Chinese Version)

《答人》这首五言诗,其作者真名实姓无从考证,一般标注为"太上隐者"。《唐诗三百首》中没有收录这首诗,《全唐诗》第784卷第14首收录了这首诗。尽管这首五言诗联间失黏,但不少选本将其归为五绝,本书从之,也将其视作五绝。

诗题为《答人》,实则诗人"太上隐者"的个人小传:读诗体见其人,品格融其中,即洒脱中见闲适。读罢二十个字,一位朴素的世外高人跃然而出,活灵活现。尾联出句"山中无历日","无历日"即"无日历",正如《唐子西文录》中收录的唐代一位佚名诗人的残篇所言:山僧不解数甲子,一叶落知天下秋。超然、脱俗之感顿生,自然就过渡到对句"寒尽不知年"了。"寒尽"应是春夏秋冬的省称,"寒尽"代表四季已过,即四季成岁,一个轮回结束了,然而却"不知年",不知今夕是何年何月。

Answer to Question "Who Are You?"
○By *Supreme Recluse*
Beneath a pine, at times I'll lie
'Sleep with my head on a stone high.
'Mong mountains no calendar sold,

I know not years though it's not cold.

Annotations to Its Version of English Verse(韵体译诗注释)

1. beneath: *Preposition* extending directly underneath, typically with close contact(尤指紧挨)在……下方

2. pine: *Noun* (also pine tree) an evergreen coniferous tree which has clusters of long needle-shaped leaves. Many kinds are grown for the soft timber, which is widely used for furniture and pulp, or for tar and turpentine 松树

3. at times: sometimes; on occasions 有时;间或

4. 'Sleep = Asleep

4. 'Mong = Among

030 ::

牧竖　　□崔道融

牧竖持蓑笠,逢人气傲然。

卧牛吹短笛,耕却傍溪田。

五绝原诗注释(Annotations to the Original Chinese Version)

唐代诗人崔道融(生卒年均不详)的这首《牧竖》中,"牧竖"意为牧童。整首诗生动形象地描写了牧童的闲适之态——烂漫、悠闲、调皮、可爱。读罢,牧童的形象跃然纸上。首句中的"持"为穿戴之意,次句中的"傲然"为神气貌,结句中的"却"意为"退"。尾联的意思是说,牧童"放牧时卧在牛背上吹短笛,牛耕田时就在溪边田头游戏"(文东,2015:207)。

A Boy Who Grazes Cattle

〇By *CUI Dao-rong*

Hat of bamboo on head, a boy

Who grazes cattle wears straw cloak,

And puts on proud airs with great joy

Whenever he sees one of th' folk.

While they are grazing, he rides one

Of them, blowing short flute for fun,

But when they pull ploughs, he retreats
To brook-side or field edge for treats.

Annotations to Its Version of English Verse(韵体译诗注释)

1. graze: *Verb* (with obj.) put (cattle, sheep, etc.) to feed on land covered by grass 放(牛、羊等)啃食牧草;在草地放牧(e.g. shepherds who grazed animals on common land 在公共领地上放牧的牧羊人)

2. cattle: *Plural Noun* large ruminant animals with horns and cloven hoofs, domesticated for meat or milk, or as beasts of burden; cows and oxen 牛

3. bamboo: *Noun* (mass noun) a giant woody grass which grows chiefly in the tropics, where it is widely cultivated 竹;竹子

4. cloak: *Noun* an outdoor overgarment, typically sleeveless, that hangs loosely from the shoulders 斗篷;大氅

5. air: *Noun* (airs) an annoyingly affected and condescending manner 装腔作势;趾高气扬;摆架子(e.g. He began to put on airs and think he could boss us around. 他开始摆架子,以为自己可以对我们指手画脚。)

6. one: *Pronoun* third person singular used to refer to any person as representing people in general (泛指)一个人

7. th' = the

8. folk: *Noun* (also folks) (plural noun) (informal) people in general (非正式用法)人们(泛指)(e.g. Some folk will do anything for money. 有些人为了钱什么都做。)

9. graze: *Verb* (no obj.) (of cattle, sheep, etc.) eat grass in a field (牛、羊等)在田野里吃草(e.g. Cattle graze on the open meadows. 牛群在开阔的草地上吃草。)

10. blow: *Verb* (with obj.) (of a person) force air through the mouth into (an instrument) in order to make a sound (人)吹奏(乐器等);吹响(e.g. The umpire blew his whistle. 裁判吹响了哨子。)

11. flute: *Noun* a wind instrument made from a tube with holes along it that are stopped by the fingers or keys, held vertically or horizontally (transverse flute) so that the player's breath strikes a narrow edge 笛;横笛;竖笛

12. brook: *Noun* a small stream 小溪

13. treat: *Noun* an event or item that is out of the ordinary and gives great pleas-

ure（不同一般的）乐事；乐趣（e. g. He wanted to take her to the pictures as a treat. 他想用看电影的方式让她开心。）

031 ::

听山鹧鸪 □顾况
谁家无春酒，何处无春鸟。
夜宿桃花村，踏歌接天晓。

五绝原诗注释（Annotations to the Original Chinese Version）
唐代诗人顾况（约727—约815）所作的这首《听山鹧鸪》，诗题中的"山鹧鸪"为"唐代乐曲名。《乐府诗集》卷八〇引《历代歌辞》：'《山鹧鸪》，羽调曲也。'"①结句中，"踏歌"为"唐时民间歌调，联手而歌，踏地为节拍，且踏且歌"（霍松林，1991：494），一直踏到、歌到与"天晓"相"接"，意为踏歌不断，直至天明。这首诗写的是春日里游历桃花村所体验出的闲适之情（这从"春鸟""桃花"等意象中可窥见一斑），以及桃花村村民待客之热情（这从"春酒""踏歌"等意象中可有所体会）。整首诗尽显大唐盛世之繁荣景象。

While Enjoying the Music "*Mountain Partridge*" by Residents of Peach Blossom Village

○By *GU Kuang*

In th' springtime season, you can drink
Your fill as long as you do not back shrink,
And birds of all kinds here you see
Are chirping cheerful far and near for free.
By staying overnight here you enjoy
Till morn their dance and song as great a ploy.

N. B. *Shanzhegu*, or Mountain Partridge, is the name of an imperial music in Tang Dynasty. It belongs to the tone of "*yu*", one of the five traditional Chinese folk tones, i. e. pentatonic scales: *gong*, *shang*,

---

① 转引自"霍松林，1991：494"。

jiao, *zhi* and *yu*.

Annotations to Its Version of English Verse（韵体译诗注释）

1. partridge: *Noun* a short-tailed game bird with mainly brown plumage, found chiefly in Europe and Asia 鹧鸪；石鸡；灰山鹑

2. blossom: *Noun* a flower or a mass of flowers, especially on a tree or bush（尤指树上的）花朵；花簇（e.g. The slopes were ablaze with almond blossom. 山坡上盛开着扁桃树花。）

3. th' = the

4. fill: *Noun* (one's fill) an amount of something which is as much as one wants or can bear（对某物的）最大需求（或承受）量（e.g. I've had my fill of surprises for one day. 我一天中碰到的意外事情已经够多的了。）

5. shrink: *Verb*（no obj., with adverbial of direction）move back or away, especially because of fear or disgust（尤指因害怕或讨厌而）回避；离开（e.g. He shrank back against the wall. 他靠着墙，往后退。）

6. chirp: *Verb*（no obj.）(typically of a small bird or an insect) utter a short, sharp, high-pitched sound（尤指小鸟或昆虫）吱吱叫；唧唧叫

7. morn: *Noun* poetic/literary term for morning（诗/文用法）同"morning"

8. ploy: *Noun* an activity done for amusement 游艺活动；娱乐活动（e.g. The craft is a pleasant ploy during the holiday season. 在假日季节，这一工艺是一项让人开心的娱乐活动。）

032 ::

钓叟 □杜荀鹤

茅屋深湾里，钓船横竹门。
经营衣食外，犹得弄儿孙。

五绝原诗注释（Annotations to the Original Chinese Version）

在五绝《钓叟》中，唐代诗人杜荀鹤（约846—约906）描写的是远离尘嚣一钓叟的闲适生活。通读全诗，颇感意象鲜明，意境通达。首联中，"茅屋""竹门"等意象可见钓叟居住条件的简陋以及生活的清贫和简朴，一个"横"字，尤其衬托出钓叟生活的安逸和闲适，"横"意为钓船在随意漂浮之中自然而然呈横向状态，犹如"野渡无人舟自

横"之意境。尾联更是凸显钓叟的安逸自在,钓叟靠钓鱼为生,一家人因此衣食无忧,钓叟还有闲暇跟儿孙待在一起,甚至还跟小孙子玩耍嬉戏,可谓其乐融融。其实,诗中的"钓叟""钓船"皆具隐逸的象征意义,仕途的不如意让诗人杜荀鹤产生归隐之心,因此"钓叟一家不愁衣食又老少团聚,让他心生羡慕"(文东,2015:206),遂借此诗表达心迹,抒发娴静中的一种属于自己的悠然闲适之情。

An Aged Angler's Life

○By *DU Xun-he*

His thatch'd hut 'djoins a distant bay,

His boat floating in a free way

Before th' bamboo gate, to which it

Grows parallel and keeps its sway.

With fish he angles for to feed

His family day after day,

Still there's time with kids and grand-kids

For him to contentedly stay.

Annotations to Its Version of English Verse(韵体译诗注释)

1. aged: *Adjective* having lived or existed for a long time; old 古老的;老的 (e.g. aged men with white hair 白头发的老年男子)

2. angler: *Noun* a person who fishes with a rod and line 钓鱼人;垂钓者

3. thatch: *Verb* (with obj.) cover (a roof or a building) with straw or a similar material 用茅草(或类似材料)覆盖(屋顶、建筑物)(e.g. as adj. thatched thatched cottages 茅草覆盖的村舍)

4. hut: *Noun* a small single-storey building of simple or crude construction, serving as a poor, rough, or temporary house or shelter(简陋的)小屋

5. thatch'd = thatched

6. 'djoins = adjoins

7. adjoin: *Verb* (with obj.) be next to and joined with (a building, room, or piece of land) 与(建筑、房间、土地)邻接或毗邻 (e.g. The dining room adjoins a conservatory. 饭厅邻接暖房。

8. bamboo: *Noun* (mass noun) a giant woody grass which grows chiefly in the

tropics, where it is widely cultivated 竹;竹子

9. sway: *Noun* (mass noun) a rhythmical movement from side to side 有节奏的摇摆

10. angle: *Verb* (no obj.) fish with a rod and line 钓鱼;垂钓

11. feed: *Verb* provide an adequate supply of food for 为……提供充足的食物;养活(e.g. The island's simple agriculture could hardly feed its inhabitants. 这座岛农业单一,无法养活岛上的居民。)

12. contented: *Adjective* happy and at ease 愉快的;安逸的

第五章 怨情五绝

Chapter 05 About Feelings of Resentment

■ **033** ::

怨情 □李白
美人卷珠帘,深坐颦蛾眉。
但见泪痕湿,不知心恨谁。

五绝原诗注释(**Annotations to the Original Chinese Version**)

这是唐代大诗人李白(701—762)的一首五言绝句,诗题为《怨情》。首联对句中"颦蛾眉"的"颦",一作"蹙",皱眉之意。"珠帘"应为珠串的帷帘。"蛾眉"原指弯而细长的蚕蛾触须,后多用于指代女子弯眉。

五绝,贵在言简意赅,干净利落。李白的这首五绝《怨情》,语言直白,笔调凄苦,刻画的是一幅怨情十足的画面:房中女子面容姣好,因怨久坐,因怨皱眉,因怨泪流,因怨生恨。此女子恨的是何许人也,不得而知,但可知的是,爱到极致则生恨——"恨"的对象既清晰又模糊,既远又近,可知而犹不可知也。在此,诗人给读者留下了无限的想象空间。

A Feeling of Resentment

○By *LI Bai*

A lady fair rolls up a bead blind,

And sits there long, her cute brows knitted.

Her face showing but tear stains nitid,

None knows whom she resents in her mind.

Annotations to Its Version of English Verse(韵体译诗注释)

1. resentment: *Noun* (mass noun) bitter indignation at having been treated unfairly 愤恨;怨恨

2. fair: *Adjective* (archaic) beautiful; attractive(古旧用法)美丽的;动人的;有魅力的(e.g. the fairest of her daughters 她的女儿中最漂亮的一位)

3. roll: *Verb* (roll something up/down) make a car window or a window blind move up or down by turning a handle 把车窗(或百叶窗)摇上/摇下

4. bead: *Noun* a small piece of glass, stone, or similar material, typically rounded and perforated for threading with others to make a necklace or rosary or for sewing on to fabric 有孔小珠

5. blind: *Noun* a screen for a window, especially one on a roller or made of slats 窗帘(尤指卷帘或百叶窗)(e.g. She pulled down the blinds. 她拉下窗帘。)

6. cute: *Adjective* attractive in a pretty or endearing way 漂亮的;可爱的

7. brow: *Noun* (usu. brows) an eyebrow 眉毛(e.g. His brows lifted in surprise. 他惊讶地扬起眉毛。)

8. knit: *Verb* (with obj.) tighten (one's eyebrows) in a frown of concentration, disapproval, or anxiety 皱紧;皱(眉)

9. show: *Verb* to make evident or reveal (an emotion or condition) 使……明显;显露(情感或状态)(e.g. a carpet that shows wear 一条显露出磨损痕迹的地毯)

10. stain: *Noun* a coloured patch or dirty mark that is difficult to remove 污点;污迹(e.g. There were mud stains on my shoes. 我的鞋上有泥渍。)

11. nitid: *Adjective* (poetic) bright; glistening (诗歌用法)明亮的;反光的

12. resent: *Verb* (with obj.) feel bitterness or indignation at (a circumstance, action, or person) 对……怀恨;怨恨 (e.g. She resented the fact that I had children. 她因为我有孩子而心存怨恨。)

034 ::

春怨　□金昌绪

打起黄莺儿,莫教枝上啼。

啼时惊妾梦,不得到辽西。

五绝原诗注释(Annotations to the Original Chinese Version)

这首五绝在《全唐诗》中题为《春怨》,作者是金昌绪(生卒年均不详)。但在《全唐诗》此诗诗题后又标注了括号,括号内文字为"一作伊州歌",这说明此诗题目又叫《伊州歌》。问题是,一提到《伊州歌》,署名便是盖嘉运,而一提到《春怨》,署名则为金昌绪,但不管是《伊州歌》还是《春怨》,诗体都是一样的,且只字不差。本书中,将诗体为"打起黄莺儿,莫教枝上啼。啼时惊妾梦,不得到辽西"的这首诗视作金昌绪的作品,诗题为《春怨》。值得注意的是,此诗尾联出句"啼时惊妾梦"中"啼时"一作"几回"(霍松林,1991:203)。

诗中提到的"辽西"为古郡名,正是诗中妇人的丈夫应征戍边之地,应为辽河以西的地区,"包有近河北省旧时永平、承德、朝阳及辽宁省旧时锦州、新民等地。"[①]

A Springtime Feeling of Resentment

○By *JIN Chang-xu*

I drive the little yellow warblers 'way

From boughs so that they'll warble not today

Because their warbles bother my dream feast,

Wherein I should've met him in far northeast.

N. B. In this translation of the poem, the "far northeast" is approximately equal to "Liaoxi" (辽西) in the original Chinese poem, which is the frontier far from Chang'an (Today's Xi'an City, Shaanxi Prov-

---

① 摘自蘅塘退士选、朱麟注《作注法释〈唐诗三百首〉》第122页,世界书局印行。

ince），the capital city of Tang Dynasty.

Annotations to Its Version of English Verse（韵体译诗注释）

1. resentment：*Noun*（mass noun）bitter indignation at having been treated unfairly 愤恨；怨恨

2. warbler：*Noun* any of a number of small insectivorous songbirds that typically have a warbling song 莺

3. 'way ＝ away

4. bough：*Noun* a main branch of a tree 树枝；大树枝（e. g. apple boughs laden with blossom 开满了花的苹果树枝）

5. warble：*Verb*（no obj.）（of a bird）sing softly and with a succession of constantly changing notes（鸟）啭鸣（e. g. Larks were warbling in the trees. 云雀在树上啭鸣。）

6. warble：*Noun* a warbling sound or utterance 鸟啭；颤声

7. bother：*Verb* cause trouble or annoyance to（someone）by interrupting or otherwise inconveniencing them 打扰；烦扰；给（某人）添麻烦（e. g. I'm sorry to bother you at this time of night. 很抱歉，这么晚了打扰你。）

8. feast：*Noun* something giving great pleasure or satisfaction 欢乐；赏心快事

9. wherein：*Adverb*（relative adverb）in which 在那里；在那方面；在那时；在那种情况下（e. g. the situation wherein the information will eventually be used 最终会用到该信息的情况）

10. should've ＝ should have

035 ::

江南曲　　□李益

嫁得瞿塘贾，朝朝误妾期。

早知潮有信，嫁与弄潮儿。

五绝原诗注释（Annotations to the Original Chinese Version）

尽管蘅塘退士编《唐诗三百首》将李益（748—829）的这首《江南曲》归为"乐府"诗范畴（参见蘅塘退士、李淼注释《唐诗三百首》，吉林文史出版社2007年版），但由于此诗符合五言绝句格律，故本书将其视作五绝。另外，有很多唐诗选本也将其编入五绝之列，如俞陛云《诗境浅说》、刘永济《唐人绝句精华》等。

据《元和郡县志》卷二十五记载,每年八月十八日人们观浙江潮时,总有渔家子弟溯涛触浪,称之为弄潮①。潮水定期涨落,弄潮儿也随着潮水涨落而"弄潮",嫁给这样的弄潮儿,岂能"朝朝误妾期"?要知道,"潮来有信,而郎去不归,喻巧而怨深。古乐府之借物见意者甚多……皆喻曲而有致,此诗其嗣响也。"(俞陛云,2011:131)转笔奇崛,却运笔自然,不留凿痕。结语看似妇人在那儿想入非非,实则情感自然流露,算是自嘲式宣泄一下心里长期的积怨而已吧,那积怨并不一定是发自心底的真怨恨。

A Folk Song of Southern Yangtze River

○By *LI Yi*

Since to a trader I'm married

In his journey he is buried

Via one treacherous Yangtze gorge,

With no reunion-ship to forge.

Ah, seeing one wave-rider go

And come with th' tide's each ebb and flow,

How I wish instead of th' trader

I could've then married the rider.

Annotations to Its Version of English Verse(韵体译诗注释)

1. Yangtze: *Noun* the principal river of China, which rises as the Jinsha in the Tibetan highlands and flows 6,380 *km* (3,964 miles) southwards then generally eastwards through central China, entering the East China Sea at Shanghai 扬子江;长江(中国主要河流,发源于青藏高原的金沙江,全长6,380公里,即3,964英里,先向南流,后大致向东流,穿过中国中部,在上海流入中国东海)

2. trader: *Noun* a person who buys and sells goods, currency, or shares 商人;货币或股票)交易人

3. via: *Preposition* travelling through (a place) en route to a destination 经由

---

① 转引自"顾青,2009:308"。

（某地）；过；取道

4. treacherous：*Adjective*（of ground, water, conditions, etc.）hazardous because of presenting hidden or unpredictable dangers（地面、水流、情况等）危险的；变化莫测的（e.g. A holidaymaker was swept away by treacherous currents. 一个度假者被诡秘的水流卷走了。）

5. gorge：*Noun* a narrow valley between hills or mountains, typically with steep rocky walls and a stream running through it（山）峡；峡谷（尤指有陡峭的崖壁和穿流其间的溪涧）

6. reunion：*Noun* an instance of two or more people coming together again after a period of separation 团聚；团圆（e.g. She had a tearful reunion with her parents. 她和她的父母团聚时泪流满面。）

7. ah：*Exclamation* used to express a range of emotions including surprise, pleasure, sympathy, and realization 啊；呀（用于表示惊讶、喜悦、同情和意识到等一系列情绪）

8. forge：*Verb*（figurative）create（a relationship or new conditions）（比喻用法）创造，缔造（关系或形势）（e.g. The two women forged a close bond. 两位女士形成紧密同盟。）

9. th' = the

10. ebb and flow：a recurrent or rhythmical pattern of coming and going or decline and regrowth 涨落；兴衰；消长

11. tide：*Noun* the alternate rising and falling of the sea, usually twice in each lunar day at a particular place, due to the attraction of the moon and sun 潮（汐）（e.g. They were driven on by wind and tide. 他们被风和潮水越冲越远。）

036 ::

何满子　□张祜

故国三千里，深宫二十年。

一声何满子，双泪落君前。

五绝原诗注释（**Annotations to the Original Chinese Version**）

诗体"故国三千里，深宫二十年。一声何满子，双泪落君前"，在《全唐诗》中冠以诗题《宫词二首（其一）》。此诗诗题另有选本作《宫词》或《何满子》。本书取"何满子"为其诗题，作者张祜（约785—约

849)。

追根溯源,"何满子"原为人名。在唐代,《何满子》,一作《河满子》,为教坊歌曲名,一作舞曲名①。歌曲名也好,舞曲名也罢,《何满子》或《河满子》源于一个叫"何满子"的人——"白居易《听歌六绝句》之五《何满子》自注:'开元中,沧州有歌者何满子,临刑,进此曲以赎死,上竟不免。'"(李淼,2007:178)

He Man-zi

○By *ZHANG Hu*

Away for miles 'pon miles

From her home sweet, with trials

She's been restricted years

After years in the court.

She sheds two streams of tears

Before Her Majesty

'Pon hearing *He Man-zi*,

A song of plaintive sort.

N. B. *He Man-zi* is a touching but heartbreaking imperial song named after *HE Man-zi*, who created it and before his execution dedicated it to the emperor of Tang Dynasty for clemency but in vain.

Annotations to Its Version of English Verse(韵体译诗注释)

1. mile: *Noun* (also statute mile) a unit of linear measure equal to 1,760 yards (approximately 1.609 kilometres) 英里(长度单位,等于1,760 码,约合1.609公里)

2. 'pon = upon

3. trial: *Noun* a person, thing, or situation that tests a person's endurance or forbearance(对人的忍耐、自制力的)考验;磨炼 (e.g. the trials and tribulations of married life 婚姻生活的磨难)

---

① 《乐府诗集》引《杜阳杂编》曰:"'文宗时,宫人沈阿翘为帝舞《何满子》,调辞风态,率皆宛畅。'然则亦舞曲也。"

4. restrict: *Verb* deprive (someone or something) of freedom of movement or action 限制……的行动自由;约束(e.g. Cities can restrict groups of protesters from gathering on a residential street. 城市可以禁止抗议者们在住宅区街道上集会。)

5. court: *Noun* a sovereign's residence 王宫;官廷;官殿

6. majesty: *Noun* (His, Your, etc., Majesty) a title given to a sovereign or a sovereign's wife or widow 陛下(用于称呼君主或其妻或遗孀)(e.g. Her Majesty the Queen 女王陛下)

7. 'Pon = Upon

8. plaintive: *Adjective* sounding sad and mournful 伤心的;哀伤的(e.g. a plaintive cry 悲号)

9. execution: *Noun* the carrying out of a sentence of death on a condemned person 死刑的执行

10. clemency: *Noun* (mass noun) mercy; lenience 仁慈;宽恕;宽厚

037 ::

怨诗 □孟郊

试妾与君泪,两处滴池水。

看取芙蓉花,今年为谁死。

五绝原诗注释(Annotations to the Original Chinese Version)

诗体为"试妾与君泪,两处滴池水。看取芙蓉花,今年为谁死"的这首诗,《乐府诗集》诗题为《古怨》,《全唐诗》诗题为《怨诗》,本书从后者,作者皆为孟郊(751—814)。这首诗,有的选本列为乐府诗,有的选本列为五绝诗,但由于此诗为"东野所作拟古乐府辞"(韩泉欣,1995:15),且基本合律,故本书视之为五绝。

芙蓉花是"荷花的别称,以谐音'夫容'"(韩泉欣,1995:15)。苦涩的泪水越多,水中芙蓉花就越发难以适应,难以生存,最终会衰败而亡。尾联"看取芙蓉花,今年为谁死"承接首联二句,究其诗意,理解上存在着细微的差异,韩泉欣(1995:15)认为"泪水多则池水深,芙蓉花被淹而死,言外谓己所流之泪更多。"也就是说,"花死由泪浅深,下一'试'便有分别。"(明代周珽《唐诗选脉会通评林》)究其实质,"言我有情,君无情,花但为我死也。"(清代吴昌祺《删订唐诗解》)但是,不管芙蓉花是怎么死的,杀手应是泪水。泪水多,则思念多,久思不见君归,则心生怨情。

Song of a Lady's Lovesickness-based Resentment toward Her Long-time-no-see Husband

○By *MENG Jiao*

Suppose we shed our longing tears

Into two lotus ponds apart.

Whose bitter drops will cause this year's

Pond lotus this life to depart?

Annotations to Its Version of English Verse(韵体译诗注释)

1. lovesickness: *Noun* a pining for a loved one 苦死;相思

2. resentment: *Noun* (mass noun) bitter indignation at having been treated unfairly 愤恨;怨恨

3. suppose: *Verb* used to introduce a hypothesis and trace or ask about what follows from it 假定(e.g. Suppose he had been murdered—what then? 假定他已经被谋杀了——又怎样呢?)

4. shed: *Verb* to produce and release (a tear or tears) 流出;流下(泪水)(e.g. He shed his blood for his country. 他为国家流血牺牲了。)

5. lotus: *Noun* either of two large water lilies 大型莲;睡莲;荷

6. pond: *Noun* a fairly small body of still water formed naturally or by artificial means 池塘

7. apart: *Adverb* (of two or more people or things) separated by a distance; at a specified distance from each other in time or space (两个或更多的人或事物)相距;相隔

8. drop: *Noun* a small round or pear-shaped portion of liquid that hangs or falls or adheres to a surface(液体的)滴(e.g. The first drops of rain splashed on the ground. 雨滴开始溅到地上。)

9. depart this life: (archaic) die (古旧用法)死去

038 ::

啰唝曲六首(其五) □刘采春

昨日胜今日,今年老去年。

黄河清有日,白发黑无缘。

五绝原诗注释(Annotations to the Original Chinese Version)

诗题中的"啰唝曲",一作"罗唝曲",为中唐时期擅演参军戏的女艺人刘采春(生卒年均不详)所唱。虽然"刘采春未必是歌词的作者"(陈邦炎,1988:162),但在此为研究方便,视《啰唝曲六首(其五)》为刘采春的作品。据元稹《赠刘采春》一诗的结句,"啰唝曲"即"望夫歌",描写了商人妇的怨情,甚至绝望到"白发黑无缘"的地步,意为"已白的头发再变黑便无缘"(文东,2015:212)。另据明代方以智在《通雅·乐曲》中的解释:"啰唝犹来罗"①,而"来罗"则有"盼望远行人回来的意思"(陈邦炎,1988:162)。

Luohong Tune: Songs of a Wife's Longing for the Return of Her Husband(Fifth of Six Poems with the Same Title)

○By LIU Cai-chun

It is far better in the old

Days than it is today, I'm told,

While this year I gain one year more

To my age than I'm hoping for.

The Yellow River'll someday be

Clear, but long failure to meet thee

Turns my hair white, which makes no chance

For it to grow black for romance.

Annotations to Its Version of English Verse(韵体译诗注释)

1. longing: *Noun* a yearning desire 渴望

2. thee: *Pronoun*(second person singular)archaic or dialect form of you, as the singular object of a verb or preposition(古英语"thou"的宾格,同"you")你;汝

3. romance: *Noun*(mass noun)a feeling of excitement and mystery associated with love(与爱情相联系的)动人心魄的离奇、神秘感受;浪漫气氛;传奇气氛(e.g. I had a thirst for romance. 我渴望感受浪漫的气氛。)

---

① 转引自"陈邦炎,1988:162"。

■ 039 ::

春闺怨　□杜荀鹤
朝喜花艳春,暮悲花委尘。
不悲花落早,悲妾似花身。

五绝原诗注释(Annotations to the Original Chinese Version)

在《春闺怨》一诗中,杜荀鹤(约846—约906)以花起兴,句句不离花,似乎有所寄托。首联对句"暮悲花委尘",估计是化用了屈原《离骚》中"惟草木之零落兮,恐美人之迟暮"两句之意,言"闺中美人为自身将似花一样坠落尘土而悲伤,而美人迟暮之悲又象征了士人坎坷失意的英雄末路之悲"(文东,2015:206)。

A Lady's Sentimental Feelings in Spring
○By *DU Xun-he*

Upon sunrise, I'm cheerful that
The flowers 'dorn th' spring, but I'm flat
At sunset seeing them in dust
Decaying slowly with no trust.
I do not pity them for their
Quick, early fall, but I'm aware—
The way of life I'm going through
Is painfully th' same as they do.

Annotations to Its Version of English Verse(韵体译诗注释)

1. sentimental：*Adjective* of or prompted by feelings of tenderness, sadness, or nostalgia 情绪化的;感伤的

2. 'dorn = adorn：*Verb* (with obj.) make more beautiful or attractive 装饰 (e.g. Pictures and prints adorned his walls. 画和复制画装饰着他的墙面。)

3. th' = the

4. flat：*Adjective* (of a person) without energy; dispirited (人)没精打采的;颓废的;情绪低落的 (e.g. His sense of intoxication wore off until he felt flat and weary. 他的陶醉感渐渐消失,最终他感到没精打采、疲惫不堪。)

5. trust: *Noun* [count noun] (poetic/literary) a hope or expectation (诗/文用法)希望;期待(e. g. all the great trusts of womanhood 成年女性的全部美好愿望)

040 ::

闺怨二首（其一） □沈如筠
雁尽书难寄,愁多梦不成。
愿随孤月影,流照伏波营。

五绝原诗注释（Annotations to the Original Chinese Version）
沈如筠(生卒年均不详,大约生活在武后至玄宗开元时期)以此诗"代征人妇之词"(刘永济,1981:21)。结句所提"伏波"为汉代将军名号,"汉武帝时路博德与后汉光武帝时马援,皆为伏波将军"(霍松林,1991:342),还因"天宝中讨南诏故用伏波事"(刘永济,1981:21)。这里的"南诏",指"南诏国",属唐代南部疆域。后汉伏波将军马援"南征交阯,有功,被封为新息侯。用'伏波营'代指诗中征人所在军营,既是唐诗中以汉代唐的惯例,又说明征人戍守的是祖国的南疆。因为征人戍守南疆,细味诗意,思妇当自北望南。而南去传书之'雁尽',其季节似在春天"(萧涤非,俞平伯,施蛰存等,2004:55)。

A Wife's Longing for Her Husband Serving in the Southern Frontier (First of Two Poems with the Same Title)
○By *SHEN Ru-jun*

To tie some letters to the legs
Of wild geese whose kind act she begs
To fly them to her husband dear
She fails, for none at hand is near.
Into her dreams she fails to creep,
For she is too troubled to sleep,
Making it hard to dream about
Him, but a look at th' lone moon out
Of th' window drives her in thought strange—
Why not run with it for a change

To the night sky in southern part,

Shining on his camp from the heart?

Annotations to Its Version of English Verse(韵体译诗注释)

1. tie：*Verb*（tying）（with obj. and usu. with adverbial）attach or fasten（someone or something）with string or similar cord 系；缚；拴；捆；扎（e. g. Her long hair was tied back in a bow. 她的长发用一个蝴蝶结扎在后面。）

2. goose：*Noun*（pl. geese）a large waterbird with a long neck, short legs, webbed feet, and a short broad bill. Generally geese are larger than ducks and have longer necks and shorter bills 鹅

3. fly：*Verb*（with obj. and adverbial of direction）transport in an aircraft 空运（e. g. Helicopters flew the injured to hospital. 直升机把伤员送往医院。）

4. th' = the

5. for a change：contrary to how things usually happen or in order to introduce variety 与惯常相反；为了变变花样（e. g. It's nice to be pampered for a change. 偶尔被关照一下还挺好的。）

6. from the (bottom of one's) heart：with sincere feeling 发自内心的(地)；诚心诚意的(地)（e. g. Their warmth and hospitality is right from the heart. 他们的热情好客是发自内心的。）

第六章 思恋五绝

Chapter 06 About Longing for Love

041 ::

赋得自君之出矣　　□张九龄

自君之出矣,不复理残机。

思君如满月,夜夜减清辉。

五绝原诗注释（Annotations to the Original Chinese Version）

此诗为张九龄（678—740）所作《赋得自君之出矣》（一作《自君之出矣》）。以五绝的格律严格衡量,此诗联间失黏,但诸多选本视其为五绝,本书从之,也视其为五绝。

"自君之出矣"为古乐府曲名,属于杂曲歌辞范畴,全诗以"自君之出矣"为首联出句,再以不同的意象来抒发一定的情感,多为离别之情、相思之苦等情感。另外,摘取古人成句诗为诗题,有时还在题前加上"赋得"二字。首联"自君之出矣,不复理残机"中的"残机",存在着不同的理解。有的理解为织布机"因其失于调理,故贬曰'残机'"（罗韬,1994:21）,有的理解为"织机残破,久不修理"（萧涤非、俞平伯、施蛰存等,2004:73）,还有的认为残机指"布未织完而残留在织机之上"（熊飞,2008:315）,恰如一幅静止的、曾为动态的画面。本书著者认为,最后一种理解更为符合诗中的"现实"。

A Poem by Imitating Similar Poems with "Since You Left Me for Your Career" as Their First Line

○By ZHANG Jiu-ling

Since you left me for your career,

I've left my loom untouch'd o'er there,

Its fabric hanging in the air.

I, day and night, miss you, my dear,

In accurately the same way

As wanes a full moon, night and day.

Annotations to Its Version of English Verse(韵体译诗注释)

1. imitate: *Verb* (with obj.) (often be imitated) take or follow as a model 模仿;仿效;摹拟 (e.g. His style was imitated by many other writers. 他的风格为其他许多作家模仿。)

2. career: *Noun* an occupation undertaken for a significant period of a person's life and with opportunities for progress 职业;事业

3. loom: *Noun* an apparatus for making fabric by weaving yarn or thread 织机

4. untouch'd = untouched

5. o'er = over

6. fabric: *Noun* (mass noun) cloth, typically produced by weaving or knitting textile fibres 织物;织品

7. wane: *Verb* (no obj.) (of the moon) have a progressively smaller part of its visible surface illuminated, so that it appears to decrease in size (月亮)亏缺

042 ::

鹧鸪词　□李益

湘江斑竹枝,锦翼鹧鸪飞。

处处湘阴合,郎从何处归。

五绝原诗注释(Annotations to the Original Chinese Version)

李益(748—829)的这首五绝作品《鹧鸪词》,一作《山鹧鸪词》,其中"词"一作"辞",属乐府诗中的相和歌辞。另外,首联对句中"翼",一作"翅";尾联出句中"阴",一作"云"。

据说,鹧鸪这种鸟叫声嘶哑,听起来有戚戚然之感。于是,古人就赋予其哀愁之意象。唐人诗中,不少以"鹧鸪"抒情,如"宫女如花满春殿,只今唯有鹧鸪飞"(李白《越中览古》),"欲成西北望,又见鹧鸪飞"(李商隐《桂林路中作》)等。"湘江",即"湘水",水名,源自广西省,流入湖南省,注入洞庭湖,是湖南省最大的河流。不少唐人诗中,湘江成了抒怀的依托。李益的《鹧鸪词》首联用的是"兴"的手法,以"斑竹"和"鹧鸪"起兴。其中,"湘江斑竹枝"又含有典故。传说尧有二女,名曰娥皇和女英,为舜二妃。据其中一种传说,舜晚年到南方巡视,病故于苍梧,此二妃闻讯前往,失声痛哭,泪洒山竹之上,竹上泪痕斑斑,形成美丽而奇特的纹理,后人命之曰"斑竹"。哭罢,忠贞不渝的二妃投身湘江,壮烈地殉情而死,所以斑竹又称"湘妃竹"。这个美丽动人的故事代代相传,引得文人墨客竞相援引。

A Poem Aroused by Sentimental Songs of Partridges

○By *LI Yi*

Over the Xiangjiang River fly
Partridges with their pretty wings,
Singing their sentimental songs,
And on both of its vast sides lie
Tear-stain Bamboos, twigs in dismay.
Its dark clouds hanging low round me,
From which road how can I clear see
My husband'll be on his home way?

N. B. The Xiangjiang River is the biggest river in Hu'nan Province, China, which exerts a great influence upon Chinese men of letters, and as an important literary image, it is often mentioned in classical Chinese poetry. The Tear-stain Bamboo (*Banzhu* in Chinese language) is a kind of bamboo with its surface pattern looking like human tear stains, which are said to have been left by the tears of Ehuang and Nüying. Legend has it that in ancient China, Yao, a legendary monarch in ancient China, has two daughters, Ehuang and Nüying, who have later become two wives of Shun, another legendary monarch in ancient China. According to one of the legends, one day in his old age, Shun made an inspection tour to the south, but died of illness during his tour. Upon hearing his death, the two wives rushed to the scene, crying their eyes out, and their tears fell onto the bamboos, forming the pattern of tear stains. Hence comes the name of Tear-stain Bamboo. After their cries of sadness and despair, the two wives killed themselves by jumping into the Xiangjiang River to show their loyalties. So, in Chinese literature it has developed into a symbol of sadness. Similarly, partridge, especially the Chinese Partridge (*Zhegu* in Chinese language), is a kind of bird whose cry sounds melancholy, making people feel sad upon hearing its cry. Over time *Banzhu* and *Zhegu* have become two of the most important images in Chinese literature, especially in Chinese poetry, symbolizing sadness or similar feelings.

Annotations to Its Version of English Verse（韵体译诗注释）

1. arouse: *Verb* excite or provoke (someone) to anger or strong emotions 燃起（某人的）怒气；煽起（某人的）强烈情感（e. g. an ability to influence the audience and to arouse the masses 影响听众、煽动大众的能力）

2. sentimental: *Adjective* of or prompted by feelings of tenderness, sadness, or nostalgia 情绪化的；感伤的（e. g. She felt a sentimental attachment to the place creep over her. 她感到一种对该地的依恋感遍布她的全身。）

3. partridge: *Noun* a short-tailed game bird with mainly brown plumage, found chiefly in Europe and Asia 鹧鸪；石鸡；灰山鹑

4. twig: *Noun* a slender woody shoot growing from a branch or stem of a tree or shrub 细枝；嫩枝

5. dismay: *Noun* (mass noun) consternation and distress, typically that caused by something unexpected（尤指因预料之外的事而）惊愕；悲痛

043 ::

江南曲　　□储光羲

日暮长江里，相邀归渡头。

落花如有意,来去逐轻舟。

五绝原诗注释(Annotations to the Original Chinese Version)

储光羲(约702—766)的《江南曲》共四首,上述是其中的第三首,故诗题亦可写作《江南曲四首(其三)》。末句"来去逐轻舟",一作"来去逐船流"。

"渡头"即"渡口"之意,"头"为平声,便于押韵;"归渡头"应为"渡头归"的倒置,意为"自渡口回家"。值得注意的是,"落花如有意"中的"如",并非"如果"之意,而是"如同""好像""似乎"之意。徐彦伯的"归棹落花前"(《采莲曲》),在储光羲的笔下变成了"花落归棹前",然后就是落花"来去逐轻舟",寓男女之间的朦胧而微妙的爱恋情感于落花逐舟的实景之中,委婉之极。

A Folk Song of Southern Yangtze River

○By *CHU Guang-xi*

By th' time sets th' sun as if into

The Yangtze River, as is due,

Young boys and girls at th' ferry meet,

With talks and laughs, to go home sweet.

Chasing the joyful boat they board

Are drifting petals, to and fro,

Like what people in love will show,

as if to strike someone's deep chord.

Annotations to Its Version of English Verse(韵体译诗注释)

1. Yangtze: *Noun* the principal river of China, which rises as the Jinsha in the Tibetan highlands and flows 6,380 *km* (3,964 miles) southwards then generally eastwards through central China, entering the East China Sea at Shanghai 扬子江;长江(中国主要河流,发源于青藏高原的金沙江,全长6,380公里,即3,964英里,先向南流,后大致向东流,穿过中国中部,在上海流入中国东海)

2. th' = the

3. due: *Adjective* expected at or planned for at a certain time 预定应到的;预期的;预定的;约定的

4. ferry：*Noun* the place where service operates from for conveying passengers or goods, especially over a relatively short distance 摆渡口；渡口

5. board：*Verb*（with obj.）get on or into（a ship, aircraft, or other vehicle）上（船、飞机等）

6. petal：*Noun* each of the segments of the corolla of a flower, which are modified leaves and are typically coloured 花瓣

7. to and fro：in a constant movement backwards and forwards or from side to side 来来往往地；往复地（e. g. She cradled him, rocking him to and fro. 她把他放在摇篮里，不停地摇着。）

8. chord：*Noun* an emotional feeling or response 心弦（e. g. Her speech struck a deep chord in my heart. 她的话深深地拨动了我的心弦。）

044 ::

听筝　　□李端

鸣筝金粟柱，素手玉房前。

欲得周郎顾，时时误拂弦。

五绝原诗注释（Annotations to the Original Chinese Version）

此诗诗题为《听筝》，一作《鸣筝》，是唐代诗人李端（约737—约784）的一首五言绝句。

诗的首联两句由于使用了专业术语——与筝有关的专有名词，显得晦涩些，但无非是赞美乐器的精美和筝女的优雅，为尾联做铺垫。"金粟柱"为筝上系弦用以调音的短轴或短柱，是"以粟米状的点金为饰的弦柱"（赵昌平，2002：274），还有人认为"金粟柱"是"用铜质做成的筝上的柱，所以紧弦"①。无论"金粟"为何，诗人旨在以"金粟"形容短轴之精美；"玉房"则指玉制的筝枕，在"筝上所设，所以安枕，因他[sic]用象牙或骨做成的，所以叫作玉房"②，意指筝的豪华和高贵，其中的"房"，指筝上架弦用的枕。还有一种解释，认为

---

① 参见蘅塘退士选、朱麟注《作注法释〈唐诗三百首〉》第119页。
② 参见蘅塘退士选、朱麟注《作注法释〈唐诗三百首〉》第119页。

"玉房"指"居处的美称"(赵昌平,2002:274-275),具体说是"弹筝人居处的美称"(金性尧,1993:318),是"写弹筝美人坐在华美的房舍前,拨弄筝弦,优美的乐声从弦轴里传送出来"(萧涤非,俞平伯,施蛰存等,2004:661)之意。本书著者认为,后一种解释有些偏颇,不太符合诗中的实际情况。诗的尾联则寓含典故,所谓"曲有误,周郎顾"①即是。据《三国志·吴志·周瑜传》记载,年仅二十四岁的周瑜,人称"周郎",英姿飒爽,文武双全,尤其精通音乐:听人弹琴,只要弹奏者出现一点小错误,哪怕周郎当时醉眼蒙眬,也能分辨出来,予以指正。此后,年轻女子弹琴,为博得"周郎"的关注,便"时时误拂弦"了,但前提是周郎得精通音律。

Listening to Melody on Zheng, a Zither-like 12-to-21-string Traditional Chinese Instrument

○By *LI Duan*

In front of th' jade sound box of *zheng*, whose pegs
Are dotted by millet-like gold,
Sits one girl fair, playing *zheng* to unfold
Her skills with slim fingers, but begs
Sharp eyes of Mr. Right who knows each thing
'Bout it by fingering th' wrong string
From time to time, which is contrary to
The normal way to send love's clue.

N. B. Mr. Right: In the Chinese poem, the poet uses ZHOU Yu to refer to the one whose attention the girl player of *zheng* wants to draw by striking the wrong chord, for ZHOU Yu, a talented and heroic man in the Period of the Three Kingdoms, is keen on music, so that whenever a player touches a wrong chord, he will surely take a look at her/him to

---

① 关于这个典故,感兴趣的读者可再参阅本系列的《唐代五绝品读与英译研究及韵体英译探索》(下卷)第十三章第二节第四部分"译例(4)"中的相关部分。

show his awareness. Hence comes the name of "Mr. Right" in the English version of the poem.

Annotations to Its Version of English Verse（韵体译诗注释）

1. melody: *Noun* (mass noun) sweet music; tunefulness 悦耳的音乐;悦耳;和谐

2. zither: *Noun* a musical instrument consisting of a flat wooden soundbox with numerous strings stretched across it, placed horizontally and played with the fingers and a plectrum. It is used especially in central European folk music 齐特琴(一种乐器,由一扁平的木制共鸣箱和众多弦线组成,用手指和拨子拨奏,尤用于中欧民间音乐演奏中)

3. th' = the

4. soundbox or sound box: the hollow chamber forming the body of a stringed musical instrument and providing resonance (弦乐的)共鸣箱

5. peg: *Noun* (Music) one of the pins of a stringed instrument that are turned to tighten or slacken the strings so as to regulate their pitch (音乐学)轴柱;弦轴

6. millet: *Noun* (mass noun) a fast-growing cereal which is widely grown in warm countries and regions with poor soils. The numerous small seeds are widely used to make flour or alcoholic drinks 黍;稷;小米;粟

7. unfold: *Verb* (with obj.) reveal or disclose (thoughts or information) 透露;展现(思想或信息)(e.g. Miss Eva unfolded her secret exploits to Mattie. 埃娃小姐把自己的秘密收获透露给玛蒂。)

8. eye: *Noun* used to refer to someone's power of vision and in descriptions of the manner or direction of someone's gaze 目光;视线 (e.g. His sharp eyes had missed nothing. 任何东西都没逃过他锐利的目光。)

9. Mr. Right: (Slang) the man who would make an ideal mate (俚语表达)如意郎君

10. 'Bout = About

11. finger: *Verb* play (a musical instrument) with the fingers, especially in a tentative or casual manner (尤指尝试着或随意地)用手指弹奏;拨弄(乐器)

12. string: *Noun* (count noun) a length of catgut or wire on a musical instrument, producing a note by vibration (乐器的)弦

045 ::

春闺思 □张仲素

袅袅城边柳,青青陌上桑。

提笼忘采叶,昨夜梦渔阳。

五绝原诗注释（Annotations to the Original Chinese Version）

这首诗题为《春闺思》的五言绝句,是唐代诗人张仲素（约769—约819）的作品。首句中"城边柳",一作"边城柳"。

首联两个叠音词渲染出一幅醉人的春景图。"袅袅"为细长柔美、随风摆动的样子,而桑叶茂盛、嫩绿则为"青青"。柳挺城边,桑立陌上,"陌"为田间沿着东西方向延伸的道路,后泛指田间道路。春日里,这样一幅图景,多么令人陶醉啊!可以说,"袅袅""青青"互文见义,即"城边柳""陌上桑"皆"袅袅"和"青青"。尾联"提笼忘采叶":一位女子要采摘桑叶,可是手提着"笼"——"一种篮状竹器"（萧涤非,俞平伯,施蛰存等,2004:813）,却忘记将桑叶采摘。这是怎么回事儿呢?原来,"昨夜梦渔阳":这位女子昨夜做了一个梦,梦见了渔阳。渔阳正是这位诗中女子的夫君戍边之地。诗中女子精神恍惚到"提笼忘采叶",正是思恋自己远在渔阳戍边的夫君的结果。诗中的"渔阳"为中国古代郡名,其治所位于今天津蓟县,一说其位于今北京密云县西南。《汉书·地理志》载:"渔阳郡,秦置,莽曰通路,属幽州。"就这样,自秦代以来,渔阳就成为边防重地,更是唐代征戍重镇。因此,渔阳后来就成为文学作品中边境征戍之地的一个代名词了。

A Madam's Fond Spring Memory of Her Husband Serving in Yuyang, the Frontier

○By ZHANG Zhong-su

Encircling city's edge, the willows wave

Their slender, slim and swaying branches brave.

On paths amid fields grow in twos and threes

Luxuriant, leafy, tender mulb'rry trees.

An' under one of those she's standing still,

With one uplifted basket in one hand,
But with their leaves green she fails it to fill,
For last night she dreamed him in Yuyang's land.

Annotations to Its Version of English Verse（韵体译诗注释）

1. madam：*Noun* used to address or refer to a woman in a polite or respectful way 夫人；太太；女士；小姐（对妇女的尊称）。

2. serve：*Verb*（no obj.）be employed as a member of the armed forces 服兵役（e.g. He had hoped to serve with the Medical Corps. 他曾希望跟着医疗队服役。）

3. frontier：*Noun* the district near a line or border separating two countries 边疆

4. encircle：*Verb*（with obj.）form a circle around；surround 环绕；围绕；包围（e.g. The town is encircled by fortified walls. 整个城由设防的城墙围绕。）

5. willow：*Noun*（also willow tree）a tree or shrub of temperate climates which typically has narrow leaves，bears catkins，and grows near water. Its pliant branches yield osiers for basketry，and the timber has various uses 柳树

6. slender：*Adjective*（of a person or part of the body）gracefully thin（人或身体部位）苗条的；修长的；纤细的（e.g. her slender neck 她修长的脖子）

7. slim：*Adjective*（of a person or their build）gracefully thin；slenderly built（used approvingly）（人或身材）细长的；苗条的；纤细的

8. sway：*Verb* move or cause to move slowly or rhythmically backwards and forwards or from side to side 摇摆；摆动

9. brave：*Adjective*（poetic/literary）fine or splendid in appearance（诗/文用法）美好的；壮观的（e.g. His medals made a brave show. 他那些奖章很是光彩夺目。）

10. amid：*Preposition* surrounded by；in the middle of 在……之中（e.g. our dream home，set amid magnificent rolling countryside 我们的梦想之家——坐落在绵延起伏的壮丽乡野）

11. luxuriant：*Adjective*（of vegetation）rich and profuse in growth；lush（植物）茂盛的；郁郁葱葱的

12. leafy：*Adjective*（leafier，leafiest）（of a plant）having many leaves（植物）叶茂的；多叶的

13. tender：*Adjective*（of a plant）easily injured by severe weather and therefore needing protection（植物）纤弱的；幼嫩的；易毁的

14. mulb'rry = mulberry

15. mulberry: *Noun* (also mulberry tree or bush) a small deciduous tree with broad leaves, native to the Far East and long cultivated elsewhere 桑树

16. An' = And

17. uplift: *Verb* (with obj.) (usu. as adj. uplifted) lift (something) up; raise 抬起；举起 (e.g. her uplifted face 她仰起的脸)

18. basket: *Noun* a container used to hold or carry things, typically made from interwoven strips of cane or wire 篮；篓；筐

19. dream: *Verb* (with obj.) see, hear, or feel (something) in a dream 梦见；梦到 (e.g. Maybe you dreamed it. 你也许是做梦见到的。)

046 ::

题玉泉溪 □湘驿女子

红叶醉秋色，碧溪弹夜弦。

佳期不可再，风雨杳如年。

五绝原诗注释（Annotations to the Original Chinese Version）

这首《题玉泉溪》最早收录在《树萱录》一书中，《树萱录》是中国古代神话志怪小说集，作者不详。据此书记载，"番禺郑仆射尝游湘中，宿于驿楼，夜遇女子诵诗……顷刻不见。"①据说但也未必可信，这位女子所咏之诗正是上述《题玉泉溪》，颇具传奇色彩。因此，后来的诗歌选本有的将其列为"鬼诗"类，有的将其列为"灵异"类。首联出句中的"叶"，一作"树"；尾联对句中的"杳"，一作"渺"。后来，"《全唐诗》的编者在收录此诗时，删去了《树萱录》关于它的本事的记载，题其作者为'湘驿女子'。"（萧涤非，俞平伯，施蛰存等，2004：1413）在《题玉泉溪》一诗中，曾经无比甜蜜的爱情如今已经难寻踪迹，叫这位"湘驿女子"如何承受？往后的日子将无比艰难，如飘摇的风雨般杳渺，可谓度日如年亦不为过。

---

① 转引自"霍松林，1991：1102"及"萧涤非，俞平伯，施蛰存等，2004：1412"。

A Mysterious Story from Jade Fountain Brook

○By *Lady Xiangyi*

In autumn, leaves turning red sway
'Gainst wind as drunkards walk in tipsy way,
Appearing to have too much drink
Of rich autumnal hues without a blink.
At night, th' Jade Fountain Brook purls
As fingers sweep the strings, glist'ning like pearls.
Here roving as she is, no more
Is her good old love she went through before,
And what'll she do in later days
To manage th' elements in a faint haze?

N. B. Lady Xiangyi is a mysterious lady who appears in an ancient China's dak station located in the central region of Xiang, which belongs to today's Hu'nan Province.

Annotations to Its Version of English Verse（韵体译诗注释）

1. mysterious: *Adjective* difficult or impossible to understand, explain, or identify 神秘的；不可思议的；难以理解的；无法解释的（e. g. His colleague had vanished in mysterious circumstances. 他的同事神秘地消失了。）

2. jade: *Noun* (as modifier) a light bluish-green 绿玉色

3. brook: *Noun* a small stream 小溪

4. dak: *Noun* (mass noun) the postal service in the Indian subcontinent, originally delivered by a system of relay runners（印度次大陆早期由人接力投送的）邮政驿站

5. sway: *Verb* move or cause to move slowly or rhythmically backwards and forwards or from side to side 摇摆；摆动

6. 'Gainst = Against

7. drunkard: *Noun* a person who is habitually drunk 酒鬼；酗酒者

8. drink: *Noun* (mass noun) alcohol, or the habitual or excessive consumption of alcohol 酒；酗酒（e. g. the effects of too much drink 过量饮酒的影响）

9. autumnal: *Adjective* of, characteristic of, or occurring in autumn 秋季的；秋

季出现(或发生)的（e.g. rich autumnal colours 绚丽多彩的秋色）

10. blink：*Noun* (figurative) a moment's hesitation（比喻用法）片刻的犹豫；举棋不定（e.g. Feargal would have given her all this without a blink. 费尔盖尔本会毫不犹豫把这一切都给她。）

11. th' = the

12. purl：*Verb* (no obj.) (of a stream or river) flow with a swirling motion and babbling sound（溪流或河流）回旋着流；潺潺地流

13. glist'ning = glistening

14. rove：*Verb* (no obj., with adverbial of direction) travel constantly without a fixed destination；wander 流浪；漫游

15. manage：*Verb* (with obj.) succeed in dealing with or withstanding (something) 处理；应付；承受（e.g. There was more stress and anxiety than he could manage. 压力之大，焦虑之深，非他所能承受。）

16. element：*Noun* (the elements) the weather, especially strong winds, heavy rain, and other kinds of bad weather（尤指强风、暴雨等恶劣）天气（e.g. There was no barrier against the elements. 没有阻挡这些自然力的东西。）

17. haze：(in sing.) (figurative) a state of mental obscurity or confusion（比喻用法）懵懂；迷糊（e.g. through an alcoholic haze 透过醉酒的迷糊状态）

047 ::

大酺乐　□张文收

泪滴珠难尽，容残玉易销。

倘随明月去，莫道梦魂遥。

五绝原诗注释（Annotations to the Original Chinese Version）

张文收(生卒年均不详，但大约生活在隋末唐初时期)所作的这首五绝《大酺乐》，诗题中的"大酺乐"为"唐教坊乐曲名"（霍松林，1991：30），属于唐代宫廷乐的一种。《乐府诗集》卷八〇《近代曲辞二》引《乐苑》曰："《大酺乐》，商调曲，唐张文收造。"此诗首联的措辞大有玩弄文字游戏之意，将"珠泪"和"玉容"分别拆开述说，并以对仗手段形成对比的效果，言女子对意中人思念程度之深。尾联犹如梦境，将这位女子的思恋之情推向了极致。

"*Dapu Music*": Song of a Lady's Wishful Longing for Seeing Her Beloved

○By ZHANG Wen-shou

With teardrops rolling down her cheeks,
The pearl-like stains remain for weeks,
Whereas with faces going gaunt,
Her previous beauty'll be her want.
Why not go see him with the moon?
Won't he be glad enough to swoon?

N. B. *Dapuyue*, or Dapu Music (Grand Party Music), is the name of an imperial music in Tang Dynasty. Created by *ZHANG Wen-shou*, the poet of the above poem, it belongs to the tone of "*shang*", one of the five traditional Chinese folk tones, i.e. pentatonic scales: *gong*, *shang*, *jiao*, *zhi* and *yu*.

Annotations to Its Version of English Verse (韵体译诗注释)

1. wishful: *Adjective* expressing or containing a desire or hope for something impractical or unfeasible 一厢情愿的 (e. g. Without resources the proposed measures were merely wishful thinking. 若没有资源,提出的解决措施就只能是痴心妄想。)

2. longing: *Noun* a yearning desire 渴望

3. beloved: *Noun* a much loved person 钟爱的人;心爱的人

4. whereas: *Conjunction* in contrast or comparison with the fact that 而;却;反之 (e. g. You treat the matter lightly, whereas I myself was never more serious. 你处理事情很轻率,而我自己却过于认真。)

5. go: *Verb* (no obj. , with complement) pass into a specified state, especially an undesirable one 变成(尤指不好的状态) (e. g. The food is going bad. 食物变质了。)

6. gaunt: *Adjective* (of a person) lean and haggard, especially because of suffering, hunger, or age (尤指人因苦难、饥饿或衰老而)瘦削和憔悴的

7. want: *Noun* a desire for something 需要;渴望 (e. g. the expression of our wants and desires 对我们需要和渴望的表达)

8. swoon: *Verb* (no obj.) faint from extreme emotion 昏倒 (e. g. I don't want a

nurse who swoons at the sight of blood. 我不需要一看到血就昏倒的护士。)

048 ::

江南曲五首(其一)　□丁仙芝
长干斜路北,近浦是儿家。
有意来相访,明朝出浣纱。

五绝原诗注释(**Annotations to the Original Chinese Version**)
谁说约会中的男女,女子不会主动些? 丁仙芝(生卒年均不详,为开元进士,开元为唐朝皇帝唐玄宗李隆基的年号,起止年限为公元713至741年)所作《江南曲五首(其一)》给出了很好的诠释。在此诗中,丁仙芝刻画了一个大胆追求爱情的女子形象。这位女子大有皇甫松笔下《采莲子》诗中女子的风采。首联交代女子家所在的位置,其中"儿"为古代年轻女子的自称;尾联中,该女子大胆发出约会邀请:"有意想约我的话,明早我出去浣纱,就到我浣纱的河边相见吧。"其中的"浣纱",原指洗涤某种布料,后多用以指代洗衣服。

A Folk Song of Southern Yangtze River by a Vivacious Girl (First of Five Poems with the Same Title)

○By *DING Xian-zhi*

In Changgan Zone, a slanting street
Extends northwards to my home sweet,
And th' riverbank serves as its seat.
If you've a mind to be my date,
To th' edge of th' river you go straight,
For I'll be there washing to wait.

N. B. Changgan Zone or Changgan for short (in today's Nanjing City, Jiangsu Province), a well-known place name in ancient China, used to be a most prosperous region in southern Yangtze River. It has particularly become a dream place of poets, who feel it a great honor to go to that place and often mention it in their poetry.

第六章 思恋五绝

Annotations to Its Version of English Verse(韵体译诗注释)

1. Yangtze: *Noun* the principal river of China, which rises as the Jinsha in the Tibetan highlands and flows 6,380 *km* (3,964 miles) southwards then generally eastwards through central China, entering the East China Sea at Shanghai 扬子江;长江(中国主要河流,发源于青藏高原的金沙江,全长6,380公里,即3,964英里,先向南流,后大致向东流,穿过中国中部,在上海流入中国东海)

2. vivacious: *Adjective* (especially of a woman) attractively lively and animated (尤指妇女)活泼的;生气勃勃的

3. th' = the

4. seat: a site or location of something specified 地点;地址(e.g. Parliament House was the seat of the Scots Parliament until the Union with England. 直到与英格兰统一之前,议会大厦一直是苏格兰议会的所在地。)

5. have a (a good or half a) mind to do something: be very much inclined to do something 很想做;意欲(e.g. I've a good mind to write to the manager to complain. 我很想写信向经理投诉。)

6. date: *Noun* a person with whom one ha sa social or romantic appointment or engagement 约会对象(e.g. My date isn't going to show, it seems. 看起来我约的人不会来了。)

7. wash: *Verb* (no obj.) do one's laundry 洗衣(e.g. I need someone to cook and wash for me. 我需要人帮我做饭洗衣。)

第七章 景色五绝
Chapter 07 About Scenery

■ **049** ::

鹿柴　□王维
空山不见人,但闻人语响。
返景入深林,复照青苔上。

五绝原诗注释(Annotations to the Original Chinese Version)
这是唐代大诗人王维(701—761)的一首五言仄韵诗《鹿柴》(柴,音"zhài"),诗题一作《鹿砦》,实为"古绝"而非"律绝",即本研究的主题之一"五绝"。鉴于很多选本包括蘅塘退士的《唐诗三百首》都视其为五言绝句,本书从之,将其视作为五绝加以研究与翻译。

山空旷而寂静,看不见人影,却能听见人说话的声音。那声音在空寂的山中,显得格外响亮。那也许是日暮时分吧:返景入深林,复照青苔上——"返景"(yǐng)同"返影",指"夕阳返照"(李梦生,2007:13)。再者,"深林中苔翠阴阴,日光所不及,惟夕阳自林间斜射而入,照此苔痕,深碧浅红,相映成采。此景无人道及,惟妙心得之,诗笔复能写出。"(俞陛云,2011:111—112)

In Luzhai, One of the Scenic Spots Where I Live as a Recluse
○By *WANG Wei*

No sign of life in th' silent vast

Of mountains, human voice is passed.

Reflective glow, ere th' sun setest,

Ent'rest the depths of dense forest,

And once again on its way there

Repos'st on th' moss resembling hair.

Annotations to Its Version of English Verse（韵体译诗注释）

1. recluse：*Noun* a person who lives a solitary life and tends to avoid other people 隐士；遁世者

2. th' = the

3. vast：*Noun*（usu. the/a vast）（chiefly poetic）immense or boundless space（主要为诗歌用法）茫茫；无边无际的空间

4. reflective：*Adjective* produced by reflection 反射产生的（e.g. a colourful reflective glow 色彩绚丽的反射光）

5. glow：*Noun*（in sing.）a steady radiance of light or heat 发出光（或热）（e.g. The setting sun cast a deep red glow over the city. 落日给城市上空投下一道深红色的霞光。）

6. ere：*Preposition & Conjunction*（poetic/literary or archaic）before（in time）（诗/文用法或古旧用法）在……之前（在时间上）（e.g. We hope you will return ere long. 我们希望你很快回来。）

7. setest = sets

8. Ent'rest = Enterest = Enters

9. depth：*Noun*（the depths）a point far below the surface 深处（e.g. He lifted the manhole cover and peered into the depths beneath. 他掀起窨井盖向下面深处望去。）

10. forest：*Noun* a large area covered chiefly with trees and undergrowth 森林

11. casually：*Adverb* not methodically or according to plan 无意地；未经考虑地；漫不经心地

12. Repos'st = Reposest = Reposes

13. repose：*Verb* lie down in rest 静卧；安息（e.g. How sweetly he would re-

pose in the four-poster bed. 他会多么甜美地安睡在四脚床上。)

14. moss: *Noun* (mass noun) a small flowerless green plant which lacks true roots, growing in low carpets or rounded cushions in damp habitats and reproducing by means of spores released from stalked capsules 苔藓;苔类植物

15. resemble: *Verb* (with obj.) have qualities or features, especially those of appearance, in common with (someone or something); look or seem like 长得像;像;与……相似 (e.g. Some people resemble their dogs. 有些人和他们养的狗有相似之处。)

050 ::

宿建德江 □孟浩然
移舟泊烟渚,日暮客愁新。
野旷天低树,江清月近人。

五绝原诗注释(Annotations to the Original Chinese Version)

这是孟浩然(689—740)的一首五言诗,基本上属于五言绝句即五绝范畴,诗题为《宿建德江》。首联出句中,"烟",一作"幽"。孟浩然《宿建德江》,诗题中的"建德江"指新安江流经建德(今属浙江)西部的一段水域,属钱塘江上游。

水中的陆地曰"洲",而"渚"则为水中的小块陆地,即小洲。"烟渚"者,乃指江中或水中烟雾缭绕的小洲,正如《尔雅·释水》载:"水中可居者曰洲,小洲曰渚。"首联对句中的"客愁新",有为客中又添愁绪之意,"客"为诗人自称,因"客愁本来存在于诗人心中,当日落黄昏,江畔烟霭迷离时,思乡的感情更切,所以说'客愁新'"(沙灵娜,1983:397)。

Staying Overnight in My Boat Floating on Jiande River
○By *MENG Hao-ran*

While 'bove the river wide I moor
By one misty land small, I'm sure
The sunset glow ignites a sense
Of gloomy air 'round me from thence.

Th' surroundings are so vast a scene
That lower than treetops is th' sky,
An' th' water is so clear, so clean
That th' moon's image in it is nigh,
Reminding me of th' same one bright
In my home where it's moonlit night.

Annotations to Its Version of English Verse（韵体译诗注释）

1. overnight：*Adverb* for the duration of a night 在整个夜间（e. g. They refused to stay overnight. 他们拒绝留下过夜。）

2. 'bove = above

3. moor：*Verb*（no obj., with adverbial of place）（of a boat）be made fast somewhere by attaching it by cable or rope to the shore or to an anchor（船）停泊；系泊；系留；被系住（e. g. We moored alongside a jetty. 我们停泊在防波堤旁。）

4. misty：*Adjective*（mistier, mistiest）full of, covered with, or accompanied by mist 笼罩着雾的；雾气覆盖的；有雾的（e. g. the misty air above the frozen river 结冰河面上的雾霭）

5. glow：*Noun*（in sing.）a steady radiance of light or heat 发出光（或热）（e. g. The setting sun cast a deep red glow over the city. 落日给城市上空投下一道深红色的霞光。）

6. ignite：*Verb*（with obj.）（figurative）arouse（an emotion）（比喻用法）激发（感情）（e. g. The words ignited new fury in him. 那些话激起了他新的怒气。）

7. gloomy：*Adjective*（gloomier, gloomiest）causing distress or depression 使悲伤（或消沉）的（e. g. a gloomy atmosphere 令人沮丧的气氛）

8. 'round = around

9. thence：*Adverb*（also from thence）（formal）from a place or source previously mentioned（正式用法）从那里（e. g. They intended to cycle on into France and thence home via Belgium. 他们打算继续骑自行车进入法国，再从那里经比利时回国。）

10. Th' = The

11. vast：*Adjective* of very great extent or quantity; immense 广阔的；广大的（e. g. a vast plain full of orchards 到处是苹果园的大平原）

12. treetop：*Noun*（usu. treetops）the uppermost part of a tree 树梢

13. An' = And

14. nigh: *Adverb, Preposition& Adjective*（archaic）near（古旧用法）近的（e. g. The Day of Judgement is nigh. 离最后审判日不远了。）

15. moonlit: *Adjective* lit by the moon 月光照耀下的

051 ::

终南望余雪　　□祖咏

终南阴岭秀，积雪浮云端。

林表明霁色，城中增暮寒。

五绝原诗注释（**Annotations to the Original Chinese Version**）

诗体为"终南阴岭秀，积雪浮云端。林表明霁色，城中增暮寒"的这首诗为祖咏（约699—约746）所作，应为一首五言绝句（但存在着争议），诗题为《终南望余雪》，一作《终南山望余雪》《望终南残雪》等。其中的"余"，一作"馀"。

诗的首句中"终南"，即"终南山"，所谓"终南捷径"所在地。《长安志》记载："万年县，终南山在县南五十里。"①背阳为阴，山岭背阳为阴岭。换句话说，山的北岭即为"阴岭"。从长安城远望，可望见终南山的北岭，终南山之巍峨挺拔，令堆积着皑皑白雪的北岭也风光秀丽，那积雪好似飘浮在云端。诗的尾联中，"林表"应为树林上表层，即树梢以上与树梢紧挨着的那部分区域；"明霁色"，雪后天晴，出现了太阳的光芒，犹如在林表镶上了一层金边。此时已是日暮时分，太阳即将落山，温度当然会因此而有所下降，再加上积雪带来的寒意，"城中"——长安城之中自然会"增暮寒"了。霁色，为雨、雪停止后出现的晴天光芒。在这首诗中，"后二句又从'色'、'寒'落墨，使山势虚化，'明'字、'暮'字明暗相映，使人似感到山头皓素一片浸淫散入城中的动势，便从高寒中见出秀伟境象来。这种营构又非心造。"（赵昌平，2002：268）

---

① 转引自"刘永济，1981：35"。

A Fine View of Lingering Snow on Top of Zhongnan Mountain
○By *ZU Yong*

View of its shady side is fine,
For ling'ring snow floats 'bove cloud line.
As soon as th' ice-cold snowfall stops,
Sunshine at dusk runs 'cross treetops,
Which adds more cold to its nether
Chang'an City in such weather.

N. B.

1. Zhongnan Mountain: Located in the southern part of ancient Chang'an City (Today's Xi'an City, Shaanxi Province), the capital of Tang Dynasty, it is an important mountain in both ancient and modern China, well known for its rich content of traditional Chinese cultures such as Confucianism, Buddhism and Taoism. In addition, many poets in Tang Dynasty prefer it to any other ones as a location for their reclusive life.

2. Chang'an: It is today's Xi'an City, the capital city of Shaanxi Province. As capitals of thirteen dynasties or kingdoms in the long Chinese history, it used to be a holy land for all men of letters. In particular, *Chang'an*, the capital of Tang Dynasty, has become a dream place of poets, who feel it a great honor to go to that place and often mention it in their poetry.

Annotations to Its Version of English Verse (韵体译诗注释)

1. view: *Count. Noun* a sight or prospect, typically of attractive natural scenery, that can be taken in by the eye from a particular place 景色;美景 (e.g. a fine view of the castle 城堡的美景)

2. lingering: *Adjective* (attrib.) lasting for a long time or slow to end 犹存的;逗留不去的

3. on top of: on the highest point or uppermost surface of 在最高处;在顶端;在最上面 (e.g. a town perched on top of a hill 一座山顶城市)

4. shady: *Adjective* (shadier, shadiest) situated in or full of shade 背阴的;多阴的 (e.g. shady woods 荫翳的树林)

5. ling'ring = lingering

6. float: *Verb* (with adverbial of direction) move or hover slowly and lightly in a

liquid or the air; drift 在(液体或空气)中浮动;飘动;(e. g. Clouds floated across a brilliant blue sky. 云朵在灿烂的蓝天上飘动。)

7. 'bove = above

8. th' = the

9. snowfall: *Noun* a fall of snow 降雪(e. g. Heavy snowfalls made travel absolutely impossible. 因为下大雪,根本不可能去旅行。)

10. 'cross = across

11. treetop: *Noun* (usu. treetops) the uppermost part of a tree 树梢

12. nether: *Adjective* lower in position 下面的(e. g. The ballast is suspended from its nether end. 沙囊倒悬着)

13. holy land: *Noun* a place which attracts people of a particular group or with a particular interest 圣地(e. g. Holland is a holy land for jazz enthusiasts. 荷兰是爵士乐狂热者的圣地。)

052 ::

行宫　□元稹

寥落古行宫,宫花寂寞红。

白头宫女在,闲坐说玄宗。

五绝原诗注释(Annotations to the Original Chinese Version)

这首五绝为元稹(779—831)所作(一作王建诗①),诗题为《行宫》,这首诗"描写了行宫的荒凉冷落,抒写对大唐盛世的怀恋以及对历史盛衰的感慨。寄寓深永"(李淼,2007:178)。

行宫,原指古代帝王在京城之外的宫殿,供帝王外出或出游之时居住。具体到《行宫》一诗,有的学者认为,"行宫"指"连昌宫,在今河南宜阳"(顾青,2009:298);有的学者认为,"行宫"指"上阳宫,旧址在洛阳"(韩成武,张国伟,1995:494)。皆有可能,因唐玄宗李隆基"在位时常到洛阳的上阳宫和长安、洛阳之间的连昌宫巡幸"(艾

---

① 《全唐诗》在此诗诗题后有此括注。另,"明胡应麟《诗薮·内编》卷六以为这首诗是王建所作,并说'语意绝妙,合(王)建七言《宫词》百首,不易此二十字也'"(转引自"萧涤非,俞平伯,施蛰存等,2004:953")。

克利,段宪文,王友怀,2005:320)。

The Imperial Palace for Emperor's Temporary Needs
○By *YUAN Zhen*

Forlorn is th' palace of th' old days,
Its flowers turning red alone.
Grey-hair'd the maids-in-waiting've grown,
And there they sit in idle ways,
Talking about th' late Xuanzong, their
Ex-emperor whose past they share.

N. B. As one of the emperors in Tang Dynasty, Xuanzong, whose real name is LI Long-ji (685—762), reigns the longest over the Empire of Tang from 712 to 756. Under the reign of him, the most prosperous era emerges in Tang Dynasty, which unfortunately begins to fall into a gradual decline late in his reign due to his neglection of state affairs and his infatuation with YANG Yu-huan, a lady as fair as Helen, who becomes one of his wives.

Annotations to Its Version of English Verse (韵体译诗注释)

1. imperial: *Adjective* of or relating to an emperor (与)皇帝(有关)的 (e. g. the imperial family 皇族)

2. temporary: *Adjective* lasting for only a limited period of time; not permanent 暂时的;临时的

3. forlorn: *Adjective* wretched or pitiful in appearance or condition 被弃置的;荒凉的 (e. g. The house stood forlorn and empty. 房子被弃置了,空无一物。)

4. th' = the

5. day: *Noun* (usu. days) a particular period of the past; an era 时期;时代 (e. g. The laws were very strict in those days. 在那个时代法律是很严厉的。)

6. Grey-hair'd = Grey-haired

7. maid-in-waiting: an unmarried woman who serves as an attendant to a queen or princess 宫女

8. maids-in-waiting've = maids-in-waiting have

9. idle: *Adjective* (idler, idlest) (of a person) avoiding work; lazy (人)怠工

的;懒散的

10. late: *Adjective*（the/one's late）（of a specified person）no longer alive（人）已故的（e.g. her late husband's grave 她亡夫的坟墓）

11. reign: *Verb*（no obj.）hold royal office; rule as king or queen 为王;为君;统治

12. reign: *Noun* the period during which a sovereign rules 统治期;（君主）在位期

13. late: *Adverb* far on in time; towards the end of a period 后期;末期（e.g. It happened late in1984. 这发生在1984年晚些时候。）

14. infatuation: *Noun* a foolish and usually extravagant passion or love or admiration 热恋;迷恋

053 ::

乐游原　　□李商隐

向晚意不适,驱车登古原。

夕阳无限好,只是近黄昏。

五绝原诗注释（**Annotations to the Original Chinese Version**）

这首五绝(格律上带有拗救成分)为晚唐诗人李商隐(约813—约858)所作,诗题为《乐游原》,一作《登乐游原》。

乐游原为唐时的游览胜地,起码到诗人李商隐作这首《乐游原》的时候,乐游原还是京城长安人游玩的常去之地。由于乐游原地理位置高而便于览胜,文人墨客竞相光顾,吟诗作赋,抒发情怀。时至唐代,诗人在乐游原上留下了数不清的诗篇,为人所称道。对于结句中"只是"的理解存在着分歧。若将"只是"理解为"只不过""但是"等转折含义带有"以今律古"之嫌了;若理解成古代的"就是""正是",此诗的诗意则完全不同了。孰是孰非,自难定论,却令诗意走向大不相同了。

A Tour in My Carriage to Leyouyuan

○By *LI Shang-yin*

English Verse(1)

Dusk comes and I feel ill at ease,

So, I tour th' spot myself to please.
There I find limitless beauties
Of th' sun in th' evening, for 'tis
Just prior to darkness when it shines
Most gloriously and then declines.

English Verse(2)

Dusk comes and I feel ill at ease,
So, I tour th' spot myself to please.
There I find limitless beauties
Of th' sun in th' evening, but 'tis
Becoming darker till the sun
Has set and nothing can be done.

N. B. *Leyouyuan* is an area of highest elevation in Chang'an (Today's Xi'an City, Shaanxi Province), the capital city of Tang Dynasty, and it also serves as a famous scenic spot in Tang Dynasty attracting men of letters, who travel there and often mention it in their literary works.

Annotations to Its Version of English Verse(韵体译诗注释)

1. tour: *Noun* a journey for pleasure in which several different places are visited 旅行;游历;观光 (e. g. a motoring tour of Scotland 苏格兰驾车游)

2. carriage: *Noun* a four-wheeled passenger vehicle pulled by two or more horses (由两匹或以上的马所拉的)四轮马车

3. ill at ease: uncomfortable; uneasy 不舒适;心神不宁

4. tour: *Verb* (with obj.) make a tour of (an arca) 旅行;游历;观光 (e. g. He decided to tour France. 他决定游览法国。)

5. th' = the

6. beauty: *Noun* (the beauties of) the pleasing or attractive features of (something) 赏心悦目之处;引人之处;妙处 (e. g. the beauties of the English countryside 英格兰乡村的引人之处)

7. 'tis = it is

8. prior to: before a particular time or event 在……以前;先于;优先于 (e. g.

She visited me on the day prior to her death. 她去世的前一天还来看我。)

9. glorious: *Adjective* having a striking beauty or splendour that evokes feelings of delighted admiration 漂亮的;绚丽的;壮观的;令人愉快的;令人赞羡的(e.g. a glorious autumn day 美丽宜人的秋日)

10. decline: *Verb* (no obj.) (especially of the sun) move downwards (尤指太阳)下沉

11. set: *Verb* (no obj.) (of the sun, moon, or another celestial body) appear to move towards and below the earth's horizon as the earth rotates (太阳、月亮等天体)落下;下沉(e.g. The sun was setting and a warm, red glow filled the sky. 太阳快要落下,天空一片温暖的红色霞光。)

054 ::

长安秋望 □杜牧

楼倚霜树外,镜天无一毫。

南山与秋色,气势两相高。

五绝原诗注释(Annotations to the Original Chinese Version)

杜牧(约803—852)在秋天里遥望长安,眼中所见正是秋高气爽之景致。整首诗以拟人化手法赞美了秋色中的长安,尤其以"南山"(指终南山)为长安的代表。首句"楼倚霜树外",楼几乎俯身霜树之上,言楼比霜树还高——尽管树已经很高大了;次句中,天空如明镜,竟然没有一丝一毫的云彩;三、四句中,"南山"与"秋色"展开比试,在"气势"上互相比高,看谁更胜一筹。但是,比试的结果未知,留给读者自己去想象了。尾联中,诗人实则以实托虚,将长安的秋色形象化地展示了出来。

Looking Afar at Chang'an in Autumn

○By *DU Mu*

The towers look down at trees high,

Which are in frost veiled, and the sky,

As clear as crystal, shows no trace

Of cloud in an expanse of space.

第七章 景色五绝

South Mountain and Autumnal View
Compete for grandeur to see who
Is grander than the other one,
And is the competition done?

N. B.

1. Chang'an: It is today's Xi'an City, the capital city of Shaanxi Province. As capitals of thirteen dynasties or kingdoms in the long Chinese history, it used to be a holy land for all men of letters. In particular, *Chang'an*, the capital of Tang Dynasty, has become a dream place of poets, who feel it a great honor to go to that place and often mention it in their poetry.

2. Zhongnan Mountain or Nanshan Mountain (the South Mountain) for short: Located in the southern part of ancient Chang'an City (Today's Xi'an City, Shaanxi Province), the capital of Tang Dynasty, it is an important mountain in both ancient and modern China, well known for its rich content of traditional Chinese cultures such as Confucianism, Buddhism and Taoism. In addition, many poets in Tang Dynasty prefer it to any other ones as a location for their reclusive life.

Annotations to Its Version of English Verse(韵体译诗注释)

1. afar: *Adverb* (chiefly poetic literary) at or to a distance(主要用在诗性文学中)在远方;向远方(e.g. Our hero travelled afar. 我们的英雄一路远行。)

2. veil: *Verb* (with obj.) cover with or as though with a veil (似)以面纱遮掩

3. trace: *Noun* a mark, object, or other indication of the existence or passing of something 痕迹;踪迹(e.g. Remove all traces of the old adhesive. 除去所有旧的粘合剂留下的痕迹。)

4. expanse: *Noun* an area of something, typically land or sea, presenting a wide continuous surface 广阔区域;大片地区;浩瀚

5. grandeur: *Noun* (mass noun) splendour and impressiveness, especially of appearance or style (尤指外表或风格)壮丽;辉煌(e.g. the grandeur of mountain scenery 山区风景的壮丽)

6. grand: *Adjective* magnificent and imposing in appearance, size, or style (外表、规模或风格上)宏伟的;壮丽的(e.g. a grand country house 一座宏伟的乡村别墅)

055 ::

江村夜泊 □项斯

日落江路黑,前村人语稀。

几家深树里,一火夜渔归。

五绝原诗注释(Annotations to the Original Chinese Version)

项斯(生卒年均不详,约公元836年前后在世)所作这首《江村夜泊》,着笔细微,描画了一幅江村夜晚景色图,是诗人夜泊江边村落时眼中所见之景。其中,首句中"日落",一作"月落";结句中"一火",一作"点火",意为"一点灯火,渔船上所用之灯"(霍松林,1991:858)。光看首联,不觉得诗人项斯所描绘的这幅夜晚图景有什么奇特之处,但尾联一出,顿时给人一种温馨之感:几户人家掩映在树林幽深之处,其中一家的主人是位渔人,正手持一支火把往家赶,也许鱼获颇丰,嘴里还哼着小曲儿呢。

The Scenery of a Riverside Village I Observed at Night after Mooring by It

○By *XIANG Si*

Well after sunset, th' road is black

'Long th' riverbank, and there's a lack

Of voice in th' village 'head of me,

Let 'lone there'll be some ones to see.

But still, few houses dot th' woods 'far,

To which a fisherman, a bar

Of lighted torch in hand, goes back

By taking his steps slow and slack.

Annotations to Its Version of English Verse(韵体译诗注释)

1. riverside: *Noun* (often as modifier) the ground along a riverbank 河边;河畔(e.g. a riverside car park 一个河畔停车场)

2. moor: *Verb* (no obj., with adverbial of place) (of a boat) be made fast somewhere by attaching it by cable or rope to the shore or to an anchor (船)停泊;系

泊;系留;被系住（e.g. We moored alongside a jetty. 我们停泊在防波堤旁。）

3. th' = the

4. 'Long = Along

5. riverbank: *Noun* the bank of a river 河岸

6. 'head = ahead

7. 'lone = alone

8. dot: *Verb* (of a number of items) be scattered over (an area) 散布于;星罗棋布于;(星星点点地)布满;点缀（e.g. Churches dot the countryside. 教堂零星散布在乡间。）

9. 'far = afar

10. slack: *Adjective* slow or sluggish 缓慢的;松懈的（e.g. They were working at a slack pace. 他们工作进度缓慢。）

056 ::

春游曲二首(其一)　□王涯

万树江边杏,新开一夜风。

满园深浅色,照在绿波中。

五绝原诗注释（Annotations to the Original Chinese Version）

可能是诗体为"万树江边杏,新开一夜风。满园深浅色,照在绿波中"的一诗太"流行",变得很"抢手"而被署上不同的作者,有的署名韩愈,有的署名张仲素,有的署名王涯(约764—835),且诗题也略有差异。《全唐诗》在《春游曲二首》题下署名王涯,本书从之,视其为王涯的作品《春游曲二首(其一)》。首句"万树江边杏"中,"江:指曲江。唐代曲江池西南有杏园,为新进士游宴之地。"(霍松林,1991:718)

纵观全诗,一幅春意盎然的春光图画呈现于眼前。画中江畔有杏树万棵(属虚指),一夜春风吹来,杏花片片开放,颜色深浅不同,倒映在曲江之水的碧波之中。

Songs of Outings in Spring (First of Two Poems with the Same Title)

○By *WANG Ya*

With spring wind blowing through the night,

Now apricots produce blooms, dark or light
In shades of single-color stark,
Which slightly sway in th' riverside spring park.
Such countless trees with blooms in view
Cast their reflections o'er the ripples blue.

Annotations to Its Version of English Verse（韵体译诗注释）

1. outing: *Noun* a trip taken for pleasure, especially one lasting a day or less（尤指一日内的）外出游玩（e. g. They would go on family outings to the movies. 他们会全家出去看电影。）

2. apricot: *Noun* a juicy, soft fruit, resembling a small peach, of an orange-yellow colour 杏

3. bloom: *Noun* a flower, especially one cultivated for its beauty（尤指供观赏的）花

4. shade: *Noun* a colour, especially with regard to how light or dark it is or as distinguished from one nearly like it（色彩的）深浅浓淡（e. g. various shades of blue 深浅不同的蓝色）

5. stark: *Adjective* (attrib.) complete; sheer 完全的;十足的（e. g. He came running back in stark terror. 他极为恐惧地跑回来。）

6. sway: *Verb* move or cause to move slowly or rhythmically backwards and forwards or from side to side 摇摆;摆动

7. th' = the

8. riverside: *Noun* (often as modifier) the ground along a riverbank 河边;河畔（e. g. a riverside car park 一个河畔停车场）

9. in view: visible to someone 看得见的（e. g. The youth was keeping him in view. 那个少年一直盯着他。）

10. reflection: *Noun* (count noun) an image seen in a mirror or shiny surface（镜子或光洁面）映像（e. g. Marianne surveyed her reflection in the mirror. 玛丽安审视着自己的镜中映像。）

11. o'er = over

12. ripple: *Noun* a small wave or series of waves on the surface of water, especially as caused by a slight breeze or an object dropping into it（尤指由微风或投入水中之物而起的）涟漪;微波;细浪

第八章 物象五绝

Chapter 08 About Images of Object

057 ::

曲池荷　□卢照邻
浮香绕曲岸，圆影覆华池。
常恐秋风早，飘零君不知。

五绝原诗注释（Annotations to the Original Chinese Version）

这是唐代诗人卢照邻（约636—680）创作的一首五绝《曲池荷》，俞陛云(2011)《诗境浅说》作《曲江花》，宋人洪迈辑《万首唐人绝句》五言卷八作《曲江池》①。另，首联对句中的"圆影"，有的唐诗选本作"园影"，有人解释为"园林中的身影"（李云逸，1998：158）。但是，这与诗意不符。本书著者认为，此应为形似致误，也有人认为"似作'圆'是"（任国绪，1989：208），这样也比较符合诗意。

诗题《曲池荷》，一作《曲江池》或《曲江花》，但"观全诗言荷，似题'曲池荷'为宜"（祝尚书，1994：171），本书从后者。诗题中提及的"曲池"，当指"曲江池，在长安……《雍录》卷六：唐曲江，本秦隑州，隋宇文恺营京城，凿之以为池，包黄渠水为芙蓉池，且为芙蓉园，

---

① 参见"徐明霞，1980：42"。

'三月三日,九月九日,京都士女咸即此祓禊'"(祝尚书,1994:171)。诗人在尾联传达出一定的言外之意、弦外之音,可以说诗人在"言外有抱才不遇,早年零落之感"(沈德潜《唐诗别裁》)。具体而言,有人认为"照邻当武后时不见用,故以荷之芳洁,比己之才美,又恐早落而不为人知也。"(吴昌祺《删订唐诗解》)

Lotus on Qujiang Pond

○By *LU Zhao-lin*

Above th' pond, floating in the air,

Its scent circles 'round th' curved bank there,

And its green leaves cast shadows round

Onto the pretty pond renowned.

More often than not, its unease

Lies in th' fact that the earlier wind

In th' fall makes it fade to pieces

Before its value you can find.

N. B. As an imperial garden in Tang Dynasty, the Qujiang Pond is of a long history. Located in Chang'an (Today's Xi'an City, Shaanxi Province), the capital city of Tang Dynasty, it has become a wonderland especially for men of letters, who travel to that place and often mention it in their works.

Annotations to Its Version of English Verse（韵体译诗注释）

1. lotus: *Noun* either of two large water lilies 大型莲;睡莲;荷

2. pond: *Noun* a fairly small body of still water formed naturally or by artificial means 池塘

3. th' = the

4. scent: *Noun* a distinctive smell, especially one that is pleasant 气味;香味 (e.g. the scent of freshly cut hay 新切的干草香味)

5. 'round = around

6. bank: *Noun* the land alongside or sloping down to a river or lake (河或湖的)堤岸

7. round：*Adjective* shaped like or approximately like a circle or cylinder 圆形的；圆柱形的；近似圆形的；近似圆柱形的

8. pretty：*Adjective*（of a thing）pleasing to the eye or the ear（事物）悦目的；悦耳的（e.g. a pretty summer dress 好看的夏季连衣裙）

9. renowned：*Adjective* known or talked about by many people；famous 有名望的；著名的

10. unease：*Noun*（mass noun）anxiety or discontent 担心；忧虑（e.g. public unease about defence policy 公众对国防政策的担忧）

11. fall：*Noun*（also Fall）（N. Amer.）autumn（北美用法）秋天

12. fade：*Verb*（of a flower）lose freshness and wither（鲜花）枯萎；凋零

13. imperial：*Adjective* of or relating to an emperor（与）皇帝（有关）的（e.g. the imperial family 皇族）

14. wonderland：*Noun* a land or place full of wonderful things 仙境；美好的地方

058 ::

宫槐陌　□裴迪

门前宫槐陌，是向欹湖道。
秋来山雨多，落叶无人扫。

五绝原诗注释（Annotations to the Original Chinese Version）

这首《宫槐陌》是唐代诗人裴迪（约716—？）的一首五绝作品，收录在王维《辋川集》中。除了王维的二十首诗作外，《辋川集》中还收有裴迪唱和的五绝诗二十首，所以诗题一作《辋川集二十首·宫槐陌》。其中，首联出句中的"前"，一作"南"；对句中的"是"，一作"堤"。尾联出句中的"山"，一作"风"。

门前有一条路，路旁长满了宫槐，谓之曰"宫槐陌"。宫槐，其实指的就是槐树，因根据《周礼》的记载，周代宫廷植三槐，三公位焉，故后世皇宫中多栽植，因称。首联对句中的"是"，在古诗词中多为代词，具有书面语性质，义为"这""此""这个"等。还是在首联对句中，"欹湖"为辋川王维别业中一处胜景，因"欹"有"倾斜""歪"之意，所以"欹湖当因湖势倾斜而得名"（邓安生，刘畅，杨永明，1990：202）。

The Acacia Tree-lined Lane
○By *PEI Di*

Before th' door lies th' lane, found to lead
To Qihu Lake, well-shaped indeed.
The autumn comes with rainfall high
And with more fallen leaves that dry,
But none appears and then cleans it
By brushing them 'way bit by bit.

N. B. *Gonghuai-mo* or the Acacia Tree-lined Lane, and Qihu Lake, are two of the well-known scenic spots, located in the dwelling place of WANG Wei, a good friend of PEI Di and a great poet in Tang Dynasty.

Annotations to Its Version of English Verse（韵体译诗注释）

1. acacia：*Noun* (also acacia tree) a tree or shrub of warm climates which bears spikes or clusters of yellow or white flowers and is typically thorny 金合欢属植物；刺槐

2. lane：*Noun* a narrow road, especially in a rural area（尤指农村地区的）小路（e.g. She drove along the winding lane. 她沿着弯曲小路开车。）

3. th' = the

4. indeed：*Adverb* used to emphasize a description, typically of a quality or condition（用于强调描述,尤指对品质或状况的描述）真是（e.g. It was a very good buy indeed. 真是桩好买卖。）

5. rainfall：*Noun* the quantity of rain falling within a given area in a given time（降)雨量（e.g. low rainfall 低降雨量）

6. dry：*Verb*（no obj.）become dry 变干（e.g. He is waiting for the paint to dry. 他等着油漆变干。）

7. 'way = away

8. bit by bit：gradually 一点一点地；渐渐地（e.g. The school was built bit by bit over the years. 这所学校是多年来一点一点地建起来的。）

■ 059 ::

春雪　□刘方平
飞雪带春风,裴回乱绕空。

君看似花处,偏在洛阳东。

五绝原诗注释(Annotations to the Original Chinese Version)

这是唐代诗人刘方平(约710—?)的一首五言绝句《春雪》。诗体中,首联对句的"裴回",一作"徘徊";结句的"洛阳东",一作"洛城东"或"洛城中"。

第三句"君看似花处",转得有些突然,由景转情,令人猝不及防。结句一个"偏"字,是点睛之笔,是重心所在。"洛阳东"为唐时富贵人家居住之地,是当时典型的富人区,属于"日暮汉宫传蜡烛,轻烟散入五侯家"(韩翃《寒食》,一作《寒食日即事》)中的"五侯家"之类,抑或"五陵贵公子,双双鸣玉珂"(储光羲《洛阳道》)中"五陵"之类的地方。"君"为"你"的一种尊称,在诗中是一种泛指的称呼。

An Ironical Thought on Snow in Spring

○By *LIU Fang-ping*

In spring, wind cold blows flakes of snow,

In th' sky flying wild to and fro.

They wave like flowers blooming where

The very rich reside—the east

Of Luoyang City, and just there

For th' eyes th' rich take them as a feast.

N. B. Luoyang City: It is today's Luoyang City, He'nan Province. As the eastern capital of Tang Dynasty and capitals of thirteen dynasties or kingdoms in the long Chinese history, it used to be a second holy land for all men of letters, the first one being Chang'an. Especially in Tang Dynasty, it has also become a dream place of poets, who feel it a great honor to go to that place and often mention it in their poetry.

Annotations to Its Version of English Verse(韵体译诗注释)

1. ironical: *Adjective* happening in the opposite way to what is expected, and typically causing wry amusement because of this; poignantly contrary to what was expected or intended 具有讽刺意味的;令人啼笑皆非的;出乎意料的

2. th' = the

3. to and fro: in a constant movement backwards and forwards or from side to side 来来往往地；往复地（e. g. She cradled him, rocking him to and fro. 她把他放在摇篮里，不停地摇着。）

4. bloom: *Verb*（no obj.）produce flowers; be in flower（不接宾语）开花；在开花；处于花期

5. feast: *Noun* something giving great pleasure or satisfaction 欢乐；赏心快事

060 ::

落叶　□孔绍安

早秋惊落叶，飘零似客心。

翻飞未肯下，犹言惜故林。

五绝原诗注释（**Annotations to the Original Chinese Version**）

严格来说，此诗为五言"古绝"，而非五言"律绝"，但有不少选本视其为五绝，本书从之，视其为五绝。此诗为初唐诗人孔绍安（约577—622）所作《落叶》，但《全唐诗》在此诗题后又加括注曰"一作孔德绍诗"。霍松林（1991）干脆将此诗视作孔德绍的作品，诗题为《咏叶》。由此可见，本诗作者的归属存在一定的争议。为方便起见，本书中视其为孔绍安的作品《落叶》。孔绍安的这首《落叶》，物、情交融，每一联都是先述物象，再以物象为基础转而抒发个人情感。

The Falling of the Leaf

○By *KONG Shao-an*

Startled to see th' earlier coming

Of autum, th' leaf starts its falling,

Reminding me of my mood

While trav'ling 'far in wind shrewd.

It floats aimlessly in the air,

Reluctant to land here or there

As if to say, "With my twig old

To part's what I hate to behold."

Annotations to Its Version of English Verse（**韵体译诗注释**）

1. startle: *Verb*（with obj.）cause（a person or animal）to feel sudden shock or

alarm 使吃惊；使吓一跳；使惊奇（e. g. He was startled to see a column of smoke. 他看到烟柱吃了一惊。）

2. th' = the

3. mood：*Noun* an angry, irritable, or sullen state of mind 心情不好；郁郁寡欢；生气

4. trav'ling = traveling

5. 'far = afar：*Adverb* (chiefly poetic literary) at or to a distance（主要用在诗性文学中）在远方；向远方（e. g. Our hero travelled afar. 我们的英雄一路远行。）

6. shrewd：*Adjective* (archaic) (especially of weather) piercingly cold（古旧用法）（尤指天气）寒冷刺骨的；凛冽的（e. g. a shrewd east wind 凛冽的东风）

7. float：*Verb* [with adverbial of direction] move or hover slowly and lightly in a liquid or the air; drift 在（液体或空气）中浮动；飘动（e. g. Clouds floated across a brilliant blue sky. 云朵在灿烂的蓝天上飘动。）

8. reluctant：*Adjective* unwilling and hesitant; disinclined 不情愿的；勉强的

9. land：*Verb* [no obj.] come down through the air and alight on the ground （从空中）降落；着陆

10. twig：*Noun* a slender woody shoot growing from a branch or stem of a tree or shrub 细枝；嫩枝

11. part's = part is

12. behold：*Verb* [with obj.] [often in imperative] (archaic or poetic/literary) see or observe (someone or something, especially of remarkable or impressive nature) （古旧用法或诗/文用法）看；观看（尤指看非凡的或感人的人或事物）（e. g. Behold your lord and prince! 看国王和王子！）

061 ::

风　　□李峤

解落三秋叶，能开二月花。

过江千尺浪，入竹万竿斜。

五绝原诗注释（Annotations to the Original Chinese Version）

这首五绝《风》是唐代宰相诗人李峤（约 644—713，一说约 645—714）的作品。李峤一生虽曾三度拜相，却过着清贫的生活。

首联出句"解落三秋叶"中，"解落"含有"解散""散落"之意，诗

中可引申为"吹落"。其中的"解"则为"打开""去除""除去"之意。如《淮南子·时则训》:"季夏行春令,则谷实解落"。再如《吕氏春秋·决胜》谓:"义则敌孤独,敌孤独,则上下虚,民解落。"高诱注曰:"解,散"。"三秋"主要有两种说法,第一种说法认为"三秋"指"三年",用一个秋天来指代一年的时光。如"眼看帆去远,心逐江水流。只言期一载,谁谓历三秋"(李白《江夏行》片段),再如《诗经·王风·采葛》有"一日不见,如三秋兮!"句。另一种说法认为"三秋"指秋季的第三个月,也就是"孟秋、仲秋、季秋"中的"季秋",即农历九月。如王勃《滕王阁序》有"时维九月,序属三秋"之说。在"解落三秋叶"中,"三秋"当为第二种说法,也就是晚秋之意。首联对句"能开二月花"中,"二月"应为农历二月,当为"仲春"时节——正处在春季之中,所以"二月"有春天之意,但也偶见早春二月的说法。在这个时节,各种花儿基本开放,此乃春风之功劳矣。

The Wind

○By *LI Qiao*

In late autumns, it blows leaves off the plant,
And causes all flowers to bloom in springs.
While crossing rivers, sky-high waves it flings,
And going through th' bamboos' grove, makes them slant.

Annotations to Its Version of English Verse(韵体译诗注释)

1. bloom: *Verb* (no obj.) produce flowers; be in flower(不接宾语)开花;在开花;处于花期

2. fling: *Verb* (past and past participle flung) [with obj. and adverbial of direction] throw or hurl forcefully (用力)投(掷或抛)

3. th' = the

4. bamboo: *Noun* [mass noun] a giant woody grass which grows chiefly in the tropics, where it is widely cultivated 竹;竹子

5. grove: *Noun* a small wood, orchard, or group of trees 树丛;小树林;果园

6. slant: *Verb* [no obj., with adverbial of direction] slope or lean in a particular direction; diverge from a vertical or horizontal line 倾斜;歪斜 (e.g. A ploughed field slanted up to the skyline. 一块向地平线倾斜的犁田。)

062 ::

江边柳 □雍裕之
袅袅古堤边，青青一树烟。
若为丝不断，留取系郎船。

五绝原诗注释（Annotations to the Original Chinese Version）

雍裕之约公元785年后出生，约公元813年前后在世。在其五绝《江边柳》中，一反"折柳"送别这一传统，转而愿柳"丝不断"，以"系郎船"，可谓推陈出新，表达了思妇难舍难分的离别之情。同时，诗人站在女性的角度，将"江边柳"这一物象拟人化，令人仿佛看见一位婀娜如柳丝般多姿的女子，脉脉含情，柔情似水，情思无限。

首句"袅袅"，一作"嫋嫋"，次句"一树烟"是对柳树特别是柳丝姿态一种瑰丽的想象：春来丝碧，随风飘拂，如烟笼树。跟张仲素《春闺思》（参见第045首）首联一样，此诗首联中"袅袅"也为细长柔美、随风摆动的样子，而春来柳枝生芽变得嫩绿则为"青青"。三四句义为"那拂扫行舟的柳条如能变成折不断的丝绳，留下来就可能用来紧紧系住远行情郎的船"（文东，2015：173）了，之所以说"留下来"，就是因为雍裕之反"折柳送行"之意而用之。

The Riverside Willows

○By *YONG Yu-zhi*

By th' old bank standing, th' willows wave
Their pliable, fine and leafy branches brave,
Which are so swaying, soft an' slim
That th' green trees seem to be veiled by mist dim.
How I wish those branches were made
Into a long unbroken rope like braid!
Then, what if I use it to tie
The boat, on which he'll get and say good-bye?

Annotations to Its Version of English Verse（韵体译诗注释）

1. riverside: *Noun* [often as modifier] the ground along a riverbank 河边；河畔（e.g. a riverside car park 一个河畔停车场）

2. willow: *Noun* (also willow tree) a tree or shrub of temperate climates which typically has narrow leaves, bears catkins, and grows near water. Its pliant branches yield osiers for basketry, and the timber has various uses 柳树

3. th' = the

4. pliable: *Adjective* easily bent; flexible 易弯的；柔韧的；灵活的；圆通的（e.g. Quality leather is pliable and will not crack. 高质量皮革是很柔韧且不会破裂的。）

5. fine: *Adjective* (of a thread, filament, or person's hair) thin（线、丝或头发）纤细的（e.g. I have always had fine and dry hair. 我的头发总是又细又干。）

6. leafy: *Adjective* (leafier, leafiest) (of a plant) having many leaves（植物）叶茂的；多叶的

7. brave: *Adjective* (poetic/literary) fine or splendid in appearance（诗/文用法）美好的；壮观的（e.g. His medals made a brave show. 他那些奖章很是光彩夺目。）

8. sway: *Verb* move or cause to move slowly or rhythmically backwards and forwards or from side to side 摇摆；摆动

9. slim: *Adjective* (of a person or their build) gracefully thin; slenderly built (used approvingly)（人或身材）细长的；苗条的；纤细的

10. veil: *Verb* [with obj.] cover with or as though with a veil（似）以面纱遮掩

11. mist: *Noun* [mass noun] a cloud of tiny water droplets suspended in the atmosphere at or near the earth's surface limiting visibility (to a lesser extent than fog; strictly, with visibility remaining above 1 km)（能见度大于1公里的）薄雾；轻雾；霭（e.g. The peaks were shrouded in mist. 山峰笼罩在雾霭中。）

12. braid: *Noun* a length of hair made up of three or more interlaced strands（将头发分成三股或三股以上编成的）辫子；发辫（e.g. Her hair curled neatly in blonde braids. 她金黄色的头发整洁地梳成一根根辫子。）

■ 063 ::

沙上鹭　　□张文姬

沙头一水禽,鼓翼扬清音。

只待高风便,非无云汉心。

五绝原诗注释(Annotations to the Original Chinese Version)

张文姬(生卒年均不详)为"鲍参军妻"(刘永济,1981:388),《全唐诗》存其诗共四首。鲍参军应是唐代一位名不见经传的参军。虽如此,人生亦有起有伏。在他失落之际妻子张文姬站了出来,赋诗鼓励丈夫:"借咏鹭以见藏器待时之志,殆为参军勉也。诗言勿谓沙洲白鹭,风餐水宿,将终老江湖,但观其扬音鼓翼,意态正复不凡,一遇高风,即扶摇而上,不让得路鹓鸿,云霄先鶱。"(俞陛云,2011:155)尾联中,诗人可能借"高风"这一物象来指代天时或地利;"云汉"为银河,借指高空、云霄。

The Heron Standing on the Sand

○ By ZHANG Wen-ji

A heron's standing on the sand
By th' river, looking somewhat bland
With its white wings flapping at times
And its clear cry sounding like chimes,
But if there is th' right wind that blows,
It'll fly to th' sky high from its lows.

Annotations to Its Version of English Verse(韵体译诗注释)

1. heron: *Noun* a large fish-eating wading bird with long legs, a long S-shaped neck, and a long pointed bill 鹭

2. th' = the

3. bland: *Adjective* (of a person or their behaviour) showing no strong emotion; dull and unremarkable (人或其行为)漠然的;平庸的;索然无味的(e.g. His expression was bland and unreadable. 他的表情漠然,叫人猜不透。)

4. at times: sometimes; on occasions 有时;间或

5. chime: *Noun* a sound made by such by a bell or a metal bar or tube, typically one of a set tuned to produce a melodious series of ringing sounds when struck 钟声;铃声

6. low: *Noun* a particularly bad or difficult moment 低谷(e.g. the highs and lows of an actor's life 演员生涯的起起落落)

064 ::

山下泉　□皇甫曾

漾漾带山光,澄澄倒林影。

那知石上喧,却忆山中静。

五绝原诗注释(Annotations to the Original Chinese Version)

皇甫曾生卒年均不详,约生活在公元756年前后。这首五绝《山下泉》,非写山中之泉,而是写山下之泉,即流下大山之泉。山下之泉,缓缓流动,汇流成潭、成河。水面微微动荡,映出了山色;水体清澈,倒映着林木的影子。山下之泉,流过石头,发出声音,哗哗作响,这似乎激起了山下泉的悔恨之意,令其回忆起流淌山中的那份静谧之情。

A Flow of Water after Running Down the Mountain

○By *HUANGFU Zeng*

On and on it runs as to rush

Into a river slow and clear,

Reflecting mountains' green that's lush,

And mirroring trees far and near.

Above stones it flows but hears noise,

And thinks of th' old, still, silent joys.

Annotations to Its Version of English Verse(韵体译诗注释)

1. reflect: *Verb* (of a mirror or shiny surface) show an image of (镜子或光洁表面)照出;映出 (e.g. He could see himself reflected in Keith's mirrored glasses. 他可看到自己映在基思的反光墨镜上。)

2. lush: *Adjective* (of vegetation, especially grass) growing luxuriantly (植物,尤指草)生长繁茂的 (e.g. lush greenery and cultivated fields 繁茂的草木和耕地)

3. mirror: *Verb* [with obj.] (of a reflective surface) show a reflection of 反射;映照 (e.g. The clear water mirrored the sky. 天空倒映在清澈的水中。)

4. th' = the

5. joy: *Noun* [count noun] a thing that causes joy 令人高兴的事;乐事;乐趣 (e.g. the joys of country living 乡村生活的乐趣)

第九章 饮酒五绝

Chapter 09 About Drinking

---

065 ::

过酒家五首（其二） □王绩

此日长昏饮，非关养性灵。

眼看人尽醉，何忍独为醒。

五绝原诗注释（Annotations to the Original Chinese Version）

这首五绝《过酒家五首（其二）》，一作《题酒店壁》，是初唐诗人王绩（约585—644）的作品。《过酒家五首》是一组五言绝句，应该是诗人王绩在酒店饮酒时，酒至酣处而成之作。

在《过酒家五首（其二）》的首联"此日长昏饮，非关养性灵"中，诗人王绩没有正面回答，而是从反面着笔，间接做了说明：今天这么长时间饮酒，喝得脑袋昏沉，长醉不醒，这跟修身养性、培养性情、精神追求等并无任何关系。那么，既然"非关养性灵"，"长昏饮"又是为何？诗人在尾联道出了天机："眼看人尽醉，何忍独为醒？"大家都喝得酩酊大醉，我怎么能忍心自己一个人保持那么清醒的头脑呢？尘世间的纷争，纷纷扰扰；社会变更之际，思想混乱，价值观失落；隋末动荡，秩序紊乱，诗人却无能为力。

Ironical Thoughts while Drinking in a Pub (Second of Five Poems with the Same Title)

○By *WANG Ji*

On th' very day I drink for long,

Intoxicated by th' white wine,

But nonetheless the drink daylong

Concerns no mind's culture of mine.

Observing that around me drunk

Are all who for the better try,

How cruel will I be if I

Stay sober there an' in though sunk!

Annotations to Its Version of English Verse（韵体译诗注释）

1. ironical: *Adjective* happening in the opposite way to what is expected, and typically causing wry amusement because of this; poignantly contrary to what was expected or intended 具有讽刺意味的;令人啼笑皆非的;出乎意料的

2. pub: *Noun* an establishment for the sale of beer and other (alcoholic and non-alcoholic) drinks, sometimes also serving food, to be consumed on the premises 酒吧;酒店;酒馆

3. th' = the

4. intoxicated: *Adjective* drunk; excited; extremely stimulated 喝醉的;极其兴奋的

5. wine: *Noun* (with modifier) an alcoholic drink made from the fermented juice of specified other fruits or plants 果酒;酒

6. nonetheless: *Adverb* (also none the less) in spite of that; nevertheless 尽管如此;仍然

7. daylong: *Adjective* (also day long) lasting the entire day; all day 终日的;整天的

8. culture: *Noun* mental refinement and sophisticated taste resulting from the appreciation of the arts and sciences 修养;情操

9. stay: *Adjective* (no obj. with complement or adverbial) remain in a specified state or position 保持;继续是 (e.g. her ability to stay calm 她保持冷静的能力)

10. sober: Adjective (soberer, soberest) not affected by alcohol; not drunk 未醉的;清醒的

11. an' = and

12. be sunk in sth.: be in a state of unhappiness or deep thought 陷入不快（或沉思）中（e. g. She just sat there, sunk in thought. 她坐在那里,陷入了沉思。）

066 ::

偶游主人园 □贺知章

主人不相识,偶坐为林泉。

莫谩愁沽酒,囊中自有钱。

五绝原诗注释（Annotations to the Original Chinese Version）

这首五绝作品是盛唐诗人贺知章（约659—744）的作品。此诗有两个诗题,斟酌再三,本书著者感觉《偶游主人园》稍微合理一些,《全唐诗》作《题袁氏别业》。考虑到诗体本身的内容,本书未取其流行度较高的《全唐诗》之诗题。无独有偶,清代吴吴山《唐诗选附注》中有类似的看法:"一作《题袁氏别业》,按诗既云'主人不相识',若题袁氏则相识矣。"①

尾联出句中的"莫谩"在诗中应为"莫要""不要"之意,但看此词本身的意义,则"莫谩"有"休要谩言""不要徒然"之意;谩,徒、空之意。

Travels to the Garden at Times

○By *HE Zhi-zhang*

Despite a stranger to the man

Who owns this garden land under the sun,

At times I travel there for fun,

Admiring its beauty without a ban.

Feeling like wine, to him I said,

---

① 转引自"霍松林,1991:100"。

"No worry for money to buy the drink,
And look into my bag instead—
Behold! How much've I got in it, you think?"

Annotations to Its Version of English Verse（韵体译诗注释）

1. at times: sometimes; on occasions 有时；间或

2. despite: *Preposition* without being affected by; in spite of 任凭；尽管（e.g. He remains a great leader despite age and infirmity. 尽管年老体衰,他仍不失为一位伟大的领导者。）

3. admire: *Verb* look at with pleasure 欣赏（e.g. We were just admiring your garden. 我们刚才在欣赏你的花园。）

4. behold: *Interjection* look; see 瞧呀；看呀

5. How much've = How much have

067 ::

闲居 □高适

柳色惊心事,春风厌索居。
方知一杯酒,犹胜百家书。

五绝原诗注释（Annotations to the Original Chinese Version）

诗人高适（约700～704—765）在首联"柳色惊心事,春风厌索居"中,触景生情,略有伤春之意。索,孤单之意。诗人见柳生青色而生诧异之情,感心中之事多多,皆悬而未决；又感春风拂面而生厌恶之意,因自己离群索居、形影相吊而生厌恶之感。在此,估计诗人高适取的是《礼记·檀弓》里的意境："子夏曰：吾离群而索居久矣。"离群索居如此长久,而未能一展心中抱负,诗人怎能对自己的闲居生活不感到厌烦！

尾联"方知一杯酒,犹胜百家书",觉悟之后的诗人想到了暂时的解脱,以一杯酒聊以自慰。此时,对于诗人而言,一杯酒的价值远远胜于百家书的价值所在。尾联的杯酒之说,也许是取的是张翰之语的用意。据《晋书·文苑传·张翰传》记载："翰曰：'使我有身后名,不如即时一杯酒。'时人贵其旷达。"结句中的"百家书",可谓"诸子百家之书"(刘开扬,1981:83),言书之多,作者之众。

While Living in a Carefree Way

○By *GAO Shi*

The fresh green color of willow in spring

Finds me in awe of dreams to which I cling,

And soft warm winds blow my mind, making me

Dislike my living 'lone to a degree.

By then, I start to know to the letter

Drinking a cup of liquor seems better

Than reading hundreds of manifold books

By authors with the same number of looks.

Annotations to Its Version of English Verse(韵体译诗注释)

1. carefree: *Adjective* free from anxiety or responsibility 无忧无虑的;快乐舒畅的;没有责任的

2. fresh: *Adjective* (of a colour or a person's complexion) bright or healthy in appearance (颜色)鲜艳的;鲜明的;(人的面色)气色好的;显得健康的

3. willow: *Noun* (also willow tree) a tree or shrub of temperate climates which typically has narrow leaves, bears catkins, and grows near water. Its pliant branches yield osiers for basketry, and the timber has various uses 柳树

4. awe: *Noun* (mass noun) a feeling of reverential respect mixed with fear or wonder 敬畏;惊奇;惊叹

5. soft: *Adjective* (of rain, wind, or other natural force) not strong or violent (雨、风或其他自然力)轻微的;和缓的 (e.g. A soft breeze rustled the trees. 和风吹得树木沙沙作响。)

6. blow someone's mind: (informal) impress or otherwise affect someone very strongly (非正式用法)给某人留下深刻印象;使某人感到震撼

7. 'lone = alone

8. to a degree: (dated) to a considerable extent (过时用法)相当地 (e.g. The pressure you were put under must have been frustrating to a degree. 强加在你身上的压力一定相当地令人沮丧。)

9. to the letter: with attention to every detail; exactly 不折不扣;精确地;丝毫

不差地(e. g. I followed your instructions to the letter. 我是严格遵照你的指示办的。)

10. liquor：*Noun* (mass noun) alcoholic drink, especially distilled spirits 酒

11. manifold：*Adjective* (formal & poetic/literary) many and various (正式用法或诗/文用法)多种多样的;繁多的

068 ::

江楼 □杜牧

独酌芳春酒，登楼已半醺。

谁惊一行雁，冲断过江云。

五绝原诗注释（Annotations to the Original Chinese Version）

这首《江楼》是晚唐诗人杜牧(约803—852)的一首五绝作品，一说韦承庆作品，见《全唐诗》第46卷第10首。但与上述《江楼》有一字之差：杜牧的《江楼》首联尾字为"醺"，韦承庆的《江楼》首联尾字为"曛"。可是，这也未成定规。《唐诗别裁集》卷十九中收录的正是杜牧的这首《江楼》，但首联尾字却为"曛"（[清]沈德潜，1979：631）。综合考察后，本书将诗体为"独酌芳春酒，登楼已半醺。谁惊一行雁，冲断过江云"的五绝作品《江楼》，视作杜牧的作品。

本来就一直独饮的诗人，在半醺中登上了江楼，结果迷迷糊糊之中见一行大雁飞起，飞去的方向也许是南岸，冲断了过江之云。诗人也许一下子触景伤怀：雁南飞，人仍未归，这也许就在无形之中勾起了诗人的乡愁。正因"登楼已半醺"，这样一幅"谁惊一行雁，冲断过江云"的人为画面，也许就会触动诗人的心弦，尽管"独酌芳春酒"，可"一雁南飞动客心，思归何待秋风起"（韩翃《和高平朱参军思归作》，一作《和高平米参军思归作》）呢？

On the Riverside Tower

○By *DU Mu*

In fragrant spring, I drink alone,

And then ascend, half-drunk, th' tower well-known.

Who scares a row of wild geese white

That cut through clouds scudding across the sky
To th' yon south bank and in their flight
Rush 'long th' same line of route as do clouds high?

N. B. In Chinese culture, those who are far away from home will surely miss their family whenever they see wild geese fly to the south in autumn. Here in this poem, the poet, half-drunk, saw wild geese fly to the "yon south bank", and most probably would miss his family, for he might mistake the scene as "wild geese flying to the south in autumn".

Annotations to Its Version of English Verse（韵体译诗注释）

1. riverside: *Noun*（often as modifier）the ground along a riverbank 河边；河畔（e.g. a riverside car park 一个河畔停车场）

2. fragrant: *Adjective* having a pleasant or sweet smell 芬芳的；香的

3. ascend: *Verb*（with obj.）go up or climb 登上；攀登（e.g. She ascended the stairs. 她上了楼。）

4. th' = the

5. scare: *Verb*（with obj. and adverbial）drive or keep（someone）away by frightening them 吓走；吓跑（e.g. The ugly scenes scared the holiday crowds away. 可怕的场面吓跑了度假人群。）

6. scud: *Verb*（scudded, scudding）（no obj., with adverbial of direction）move fast in a straight line because or as if driven by the wind 飞奔；疾行；急驰（e.g. We lie watching the clouds scudding across the sky. 我们躺着观看云飞掠天空。）

7. yon: *Determiner & Adverb* yonder; that 彼处；那边（e.g. There's some big ranches yon side of the Sierra. 内华达山的另一侧有一些大牧场。）

8. 'long = along

069 ::

劝酒　□于武陵

劝君金屈卮，满酌不须辞。
花发多风雨，人生足别离。

五绝原诗注释（Annotations to the Original Chinese Version）

这首诗是中晚唐诗人于武陵（约788—约852）创作的五绝作品

《劝酒》。此诗情真意切,以理服人,可谓劝酒诗中的佳作。

首联开门见山,直击主题:"劝君金屈卮"——劝君饮酒,要用"金屈卮"来劝酒。这里的"金屈卮",是古代一种饮酒用的杯子,杯柄弯曲,杯身饰金或为金质,尽显高贵之气。用如此名贵的金尊劝君喝酒,尊重之余不失尊严;用如此名贵的金尊劝君饮酒,君自当"满酌不须辞"了。

Urging You to Drink

○By *YU Wu-ling*

A golden mug of curv'd handle in hand,

I urge you to the full to drink

Without expecting you aside to stand,

Saying you can't without a blink—

Through th' elements in full blossom plants grow,

And countless partings to life flow.

Annotations to Its Version of English Verse(韵体译诗注释)

1. urge:*Verb* [with obj. and usu. infinitive] try earnestly or persistently to persuade (someone) to do something 力劝;恳求(e.g. He urged her to come and stay with us. 他劝她过来和我们同住。)

2. golden:*Adjective* made or consisting of gold 金制的;含金的(e.g. a golden crown 金冠)

3. mug:*Noun* a large cup, typically cylindrical and with a handle and used without a saucer(圆筒形有柄)大杯

4. curv'd = curved

5. to the full:to the greatest possible extent 彻底地;充分地

6. stand aside:take no action to prevent, or not involve oneself in, something that is happening 站开;让开(e.g. The army had stood aside as the monarchy fell. 军队在君主政体垮台的时候袖手旁观。)

7. blink:*Noun* (figurative) a moment's hesitation (比喻用法)片刻的犹豫;举棋不定(e.g. Feargal would have given her all this without a blink. 费尔盖尔本会毫不犹豫把这一切都给她。)

8. th' = the

9. element: *Noun* (the elements) the weather, especially strong winds, heavy rain, and other kinds of bad weather（尤指强风、暴雨等恶劣）天气（e. g. There was no barrier against the elements. 没有阻挡这些自然力的东西。）

10. blossom: *Noun* a flower or a mass of flowers, especially on a tree or bush（尤指树上的）花朵；花簇（e. g. The slopes were ablaze with almond blossom. 山坡上盛开着扁桃树花。）

11. parting: *Noun* (count noun) a leave-taking or departure 分离；分开（e. g. anguished partings at railway stations 在火车站的痛苦离别）

070 ::

招东邻　□白居易
小榼二升酒，新簟六尺床。
能来夜话否？池畔欲秋凉。

五绝原诗注释（Annotations to the Original Chinese Version）

白居易（772—846）在《招东邻》一诗中所传达出的情谊跟《问刘十九》（参见第019首）一诗一样，同时也是一首饮酒类五绝。首联人对，但首句不入韵。"榼"（kē）为古代盛酒的器具，"簟"（diàn）指用竹子编成的席子或垫子，"升""尺"分别为古代容积和长度的计量单位。尾联出句中，诗人白居易向东邻友人发出了邀请，邀请邻居前来饮酒夜谈；尾联对句则道出了部分缘由，趁池畔尚未见秋天凉意，即还处于夏热的尾声阶段，前来饮酒叙谈，也好纳凉消暑。可谓用语朴素，情真意切！

An Invitation to My Eastern Neighbour for a Drink
○By *BAI Ju-yi*

The vessel small abounds with wine,
And th' long bamboo mat new is fine.
"Would you come for a drink at night
While talking mutually alright
On th' bank of th' pond outside before
The autumn cold casts its frost hoar?"

Annotations to Its Version of English Verse（韵体译诗注释）

1. vessel：*Noun* a hollow container, especially one used to hold liquid, such as a bowl or cask 容器；器皿（尤指装液体的，如碗、桶）

2. abound：Verb (abound in/with) have in large numbers or amounts 富于；充满（e. g. This area abounds with caravan sites. 这个地区到处是大篷车队的营地。）

3. th' = the

4. bamboo：*Noun* (mass noun) a giant woody grass which grows chiefly in the tropics, where it is widely cultivated 竹；竹子

5. mat：*Noun* a piece of protective material placed on a floor, in particular （尤指）垫子或席子

6. fine：*Adjective* of very high quality 优质的；高品质的

7. alright = all right

8. hoar：*Adjective* greyish white; grey or grey-haired with age 灰白的；花白的；花白头发的

071 ::

三月晦日送客　□崔橹

野酌乱无巡,送君兼送春。
明年春色至,莫作未归人。

五绝原诗注释（Annotations to the Original Chinese Version）

晚唐诗人崔橹（生卒年均不详）所作《三月晦日送客》[①]，诗题中的"晦日"是中国古代对每个月（当然应该是中国的旧历——农历或者夏历，而不是现代的阳历）最后一天的叫法。这一天,人们出外郊游、野餐、饮酒,写这一日场景的古诗特别是唐诗也比较多。"三月晦日"是旧历三月的最后一天,基本上属于春天的尾声了。但这一天,诗人饮酒的目的却是送客,就是通常所说的为友人饯行,而非纯粹的

---

① 《全唐诗》第471卷第3首为此诗,诗体完全相同,诗题为"春晦送客（一作三月晦日郊外送客）",作者却变成了雍裕之。本书视其为崔橹的作品加以翻译研究。

郊游和野餐。正常的饮酒是酒过一巡、二巡、三巡等,但这次送客是在野外(野酌),也许是郊外饮酒,而且酒饮得"乱无巡"。也就是说,主客在推杯换盏间不知道酒已过多少巡了,可见真挚的情谊。又因上述"三月晦日"基本属于春天的尾声,所以此次宴饮既"送君"又"送春",期望明年春来之际,友人也随春天一同归来。可谓"迎君兼迎春",愿君"莫作未归人"。

Wishes before Bidding a Farewell to My Friend at the Ending of Spring

○By *CUI Lu*

At th' outdoor party, I say bye
To both him and the ending spring
As massive 'mount of wine we try
To drain, indulging in th' brief fling.
"Well, cheers——" say I. "You'd better come
Back with the spring next year, my chum!"

Annotations to Its Version of English Verse（韵体译诗注释）

1. wish: *Noun*（usu. wishes）an expression of such a desire, typically in the form of a request or instruction 请求;要求（e.g. She must carry out her late father's wishes. 她必须实现先父的遗愿。）

2. farewell: *Noun* an act of parting or of marking someone's departure 道别;告别;辞行;饯行（e.g. The dinner had been arranged as a farewell. 安排这顿饭是为了饯行。）

3. th' = the

4. bye = goodbye

5. 'mount = amount

6. drain: *Verb*（of a person）drink the entire contents of（a glass or other container）喝干;喝光（杯子等）中的液体（e.g. He seized the Scotch set before him and drained it. 他抓起面前的苏格兰威士忌一饮而尽。）

7. indulge: *Verb* [no obj.]（indulge in）allow oneself to enjoy the pleasure of 陶醉于;享受（e.g. We indulged in a cream tea. 我们享用奶油茶点。）

8. fling: *Noun* a short period of enjoyment or wild behaviour 一时的纵情欢乐

（或放纵）(e.g. one final fling before a tranquil retirement 平静引退前最后一次的纵情玩乐)。

9. well：*Exclamation* used to mark the end of a conversation or activity（表示结束对话或活动）好；好啦（e.g. Well, cheers, Tom—I must fly. 好啦,高兴点,汤姆——我得走了。）

10. chum：*Noun* a close friend 密友；好友

072 ::

劝陆三饮酒　□戴叔伦

寒郊好天气,劝酒莫辞频。

扰扰钟陵市,无穷不醉人。

五绝原诗注释（Annotations to the Original Chinese Version）

诗题所提"陆三",应为诗人戴叔伦(732—789)的一位陆姓好友,在其家族中排行老三,故谓"陆三"。尾联中,"扰扰"为混乱、喧闹之意；"钟陵"为随代所置之县,后被废除,唐初又置,不久并入南昌县,所以在古代特别是唐代,"钟陵"也用来指代南昌,是著名的滕王阁所在地。诗人戴叔伦劝好友陆三饮酒,大有反"众人皆醉我独醒"之意：熙攘纷扰的钟陵市,清醒的人不计其数,我们何不一醉方休呢？

Urging My Friend LU San to Drink

○By *DAI Shu-lun*

In cold time, it's so fine a day

For outing 'round the city to drink,

And I urge him in every way

To drain his wine without a blink.

"Why not?" I say. "There are a lot

Of Zhongling City people who

Stay sober in th' closed city fraught

With chaos, noise and things untrue."

N. B. Zhongling City：It is approximately today's Nanchang City, the capital city of Jiangxi Province. Just like Chang'an, it used to be a holy land for all men of letters and a dream place of poets, who feel it a great honor to go to that place and often mention it in their poetry.

Annotations to Its Version of English Verse(韵体译诗注释)

1. urge: *Verb* [with obj. and usu. infinitive] try earnestly or persistently to persuade (someone) to do something 力劝;恳求 (e.g. He urged her to come and stay with us. 他劝她过来和我们同住。)

2. outing: *Noun* a trip taken for pleasure, especially one lasting a day or less (尤指一日内的)外出游玩 (e.g. They would go on family outings to the movies. 他们会全家出去看电影。)

3. 'round = around

4. drain: *Verb* (of a person) drink the entire contents of (a glass or other container) 喝干;喝光(杯子等)中的液体 (e.g. He seized the Scotch set before him and drained it. 他抓起面前的苏格兰威士忌一饮而尽。)

5. blink: *Noun* (figurative) a moment's hesitation (比喻用法)片刻的犹豫;举棋不定 (e.g. Feargal would have given her all this without a blink. 费尔盖尔本会毫不犹豫把这一切给她。)

6. sober: *Adjective* (soberer, soberest) not affected by alcohol; not drunk 未醉的;清醒的

7. th' = the

8. fraught: *Adjective* [predic.] (fraught with) (of a situation or course of action) filled with or destined to result in (something undesirable) (情形或行动过程)充满(令人不快之事)的;注定导致(令人不快之事)的 (e.g. Marketing any new product is fraught with danger. 销售任何新产品都有很大风险。)

9. chaos: *Noun* [mass noun] complete disorder and confusion 混乱 (e.g. Snow caused chaos in the region. 降雪在当地引起了混乱。)

第十章 月夜五绝

Chapter 10 About Moonlit Nights

073 ::

中秋月二首(其二)　□李峤

圆魄上寒空,皆言四海同。

安知千里外,不有雨兼风?

五绝原诗注释(Annotations to the Original Chinese Version)

颇有意思的是,跟前述《渡汉江》一样,这首诗在《全唐诗》中也存在着作者之争。《全唐诗》第61卷第24首为本诗,诗题为《中秋月二首"(其二),署名为李峤(约644—713,一说约645—714)。无独有偶,《全唐诗》第639卷第23首收录的也是本诗,诗题则为《对月二首》(其一),署名为张乔。另外,其他唐诗选本中,诗题为《中秋月二首》的,署名一般为李峤;诗题为《对月二首》的,署名则一般为张乔。为方便起见,本书视诗体为"圆魄上寒空,皆言四海同。安知千里外,不有雨兼风"的这首诗为李峤的作品《中秋月二首(其二)》。其一为:

盈缺青冥外,东风万古吹。

何人种丹桂,不长出轮枝。

在《中秋月二首(其二)》中,李峤巧借中秋月这一意象,在中秋月夜表达自己非同凡响的哲思。

Full Moon of Mid-autumn Festival Night（Second of Two Poems with the Same Title）

○By *LI Qiao*

As it hangs cold above th' night sky,

The full moon's thought to be seen by

All who're within the country's land,

Where'er in th' even they should stand.

But do they know some place far 'way

Where wind an' rain is under way?

Annotations to Its Version of English Verse（韵体译诗注释）

1. th' = the

2. moon's = moon is

3. where'er = wherever

4. even：*Noun*（archaic or poetic/literary）（古旧用法或诗/文用法）the end of the day; evening 黄昏；傍晚（e.g. Bring it to my house this even. 今晚把它带到我家里来。）

5. some：*Determiner* used to refer to someone or something that is unknown or unspecified 某个（e.g. She married some newspaper magnate twice her age. 她嫁给了某个年纪大她一倍的报界巨头。）

6. 'way = away

7. an' = and

8. be under way：have started and be now progressing or taking place 已着手；在进行中（e.g. A major search is under way to find the escaped prisoners. 大规模搜捕逃犯的行动已经开始。）

074 ::

拜新月　□李端

开帘见新月，便即下阶拜。

细语人不闻，北风吹裙带。

五绝原诗注释（Annotations to the Original Chinese Version）

《全唐诗》第286卷第58首为本诗,诗题为《拜新月（一作耿湋诗）》,署名为李端（约737—约784）。无独有偶,《全唐诗》第269卷第55首收录的也是本诗,诗题为《拜新月（一作李端诗）》,署名则为耿湋。为方便起见,本书视诗体为"开帘见新月,便即下阶拜。细语人不闻,北风吹裙带"的这首诗为李端的作品《拜新月》。另外,首联对句"便即",一作"即便";尾联对句"裙带",一作"罗带"。

中国古代妇女有拜月的传统,宫廷女子和民间女子皆不例外,特别是在农历七月初七拜月的传统最为盛行,所以女子拜月也叫拜新月。据说,拜新月时,女子都要在自家庭园摆上水果和面点,点香燃烛,虔诚祷告、叩拜,如同今人生日仪式上女子吹灭蜡烛时许愿一般。古代女子叩拜时祷告,对月述说心事,祈求爱情如意、婚姻幸福、家人团圆等。这种拜新月的传统,到了唐朝极为盛行。

Praying to the Crescent Moon

○By *LI Duan*

Throughout the curtain rais'd to stay,

The moment she beholds a moon

Of crescent shape, th' young lady soon

Steps quickly down th' doorsteps to pray.

Her prayer is too low to hear;

However her skirt's laces fly

Trembling in th' north wind cold and dry,

Which can be heard and seen quite clear.

Annotations to Its Version of English Verse（韵体译诗注释）

1. pray: *Verb* [no obj.] address a solemn request or expression of thanks to a deity or other object of worship 祈祷;做祷告;祈求

2. crescent: *Noun* the curved sickle shape of the waxing or waning moon 月牙形;新月形;弦月形;（月亮）镰刀形

3. rais'd = raised

4. behold: *Verb* [with obj.] [often in imperative] (archaic or poetic/literary)

see or observe (someone or something, especially of remarkable or impressive nature) (古旧用法或诗/文用法)看;观看(尤指看非凡的或感人的人或事物) (e.g. Behold your lord and prince! 看国王和王子!)

5. th' = the

6. doorstep: *Noun* a step leading up to the outer door of a house 门阶

7. prayer: *Noun* a solemn request for help or expression of thanks addressed to God or an object of worship 祷告;祈祷;祷文;祷辞(e.g. I'll say a prayer for him. 我将为他祷告。)

075 ::

玉台体十二首(其十) □权德舆

独自披衣坐,更深月露寒。

隔帘肠欲断,争敢下阶看。

五绝原诗注释(Annotations to the Original Chinese Version)

这首诗为中唐诗人权德舆(759—818)的《玉台体》。此诗题下共有十二首,诗体为"独自披衣坐,更深月露寒。隔帘肠欲断,争敢下阶看"的这一首是其中的第十首。

首联"独自披衣坐,更深月露寒",揭示诗中主人(应是一位年轻的女子)孤枕难眠的情形。不成眠,便独自披上衣服坐了起来,见屋外明月高悬,也许是一轮满月。此时,夜已深,至少应是午夜时分了,因古时候一夜分五更,"更深"则应是在三更或者三更以后了。在这种情况之下,隔着一层朦胧的帘子看到外面月色明亮,就已经肝肠欲寸断,怎么还有胆量走下门前的台阶,到外面将月亮一览无余呢?尾联"隔帘肠欲断,争敢下阶看",意即在此。在古诗、词、曲中,"争"多为"怎么、如何"之意。

Yutai-style Love Poetry (Tenth of Twelve Poems with the Same Title)

○By *QUAN De-yu*

'Lone, up she sits in bed, an' then

On slips her coat in th' small hours when

She senses th' bright moon shining where
Cold dew drops glistening in th' air.
Almost heart-broken seeing it
Through th' little chinks of th' blind, how dare
She step down th' doorsteps with true grit
To have a close look at th' moon fair?

N. B. "*Yutai* Style" is a kind of poetic style usually adopted by ancient Chinese poets to describe love affairs especially from the perspective of a lady. In both ancient and modern China, the moon, be it a bright one or a full one, will always provoke people into various thinking. The full moon in particular always arouses in persons a sense of reunion with their sweetheart, spouse or family.

Annotations to Its Version of English Verse（韵体译诗注释）

1. 'Lone = Alone

2. sit up（sit someone up）：move（or cause someone to move）from a lying or slouching to a sitting position 坐直；使坐起（e.g. Amy sat up and rubbed her eyes. 艾米坐了起来，擦了擦眼睛。）

3. an' = and

4. slip sth on：to put clothes or shoes on quickly and easily 迅速轻易地穿上（e.g. Hold on, I'll just slip my coat on, then I'll be ready. 等一下，我披上外衣就好了。）

5. th' = the

6. small hours：*Plural Noun*（the small hours）the early hours of the morning after midnight 凌晨时分（e.g. She returned in the small hours. 她凌晨才回来。）

7. sense：*Verb*［with obj.］perceive by a sense or senses 感觉到；觉察到（e.g. With the first frost, they could sense a change in the days. 随着第一场霜降，他们能感觉到气候的变化。）

8. dew：*Noun*［mass noun］tiny drops of water that form on cool surfaces at night, when atmospheric vapour condenses 露；露滴；露水

9. glisten：*Verb*［no obj.］（of something wet or greasy）shine；glitter（潮湿或油腻的东西）闪闪发光；闪闪发亮（e.g. His cheeks glistened with tears. 他的脸

颊因流泪而闪闪发亮。)

10. chink: Noun a narrow opening or crack, typically one that admits light(尤指透光的)裂口;裂缝

11. blind: Noun a screen for a window, especially one on a roller or made of slats 窗帘(尤指卷帘或百叶窗)(e. g. She pulled down the blinds. 她拉下窗帘。)

12. doorstep: Noun a step leading up to the outer door of a house 门阶

13. grit: Noun courage and resolve; strength of character 勇气;决心;坚毅;坚定(e. g. He displayed the true grit of the navy pilot he used to be. 他曾经当过海军领航员,表现出了这一职业所特有的勇气和坚毅。)

14. fair: Adjective (archaic) beautiful; attractive(古旧用法)美丽的;动人的;有魅力的(e. g. the fairest of her daughters 她的女儿中最漂亮的一位)

076 ::

芦花　□雍裕之
夹岸复连沙,枝枝摇浪花。
月明浑似雪,无处认渔家。

五绝原诗注释(Annotations to the Original Chinese Version)

此诗为唐代诗人雍裕之(约公元785年后出生,约公元813年前后在世)的五言绝句《芦花》。全诗主题突出,生动而形象地展现了芦花的姿态和给人的感受。

从远处看,片片芦花"夹岸复连沙,枝枝摇浪花"。水岸的两边芦苇茂盛,开满芦花,芦苇生长态势极旺,还与沙洲或水边的沙丘连到了一起。每一枝芦苇都顶着一簇毛茸茸的花,芦花随风上下起伏,犹如浪花滚滚向前涌动。从高处看,明亮的月光之下,片片芦花"浑似雪"——完全(简直)像皑皑白雪,隐匿了渔家的所在,一切尽在虚无缥缈之中,也看不到在水面摇来晃去的渔家小船,让人无从辨别渔家到底在哪里。

Reed Spikes

○By *YONG Yu-zhi*

With th' bank in between, they link th' hursts,
Waving in th' wind like wavy bursts.

But with th' bright moon shining, they're foam

Of snow, veiling fishermen's home.

Annotations to Its Version of English Verse（韵体译诗注释）

1. reed：*Noun* a tall, slender-leaved plant of the grass family, which grows in water or on marshy ground 芦苇

2. spike：*Noun*（Botany）a flower cluster formed of many flower heads attached directly to a long stem（植物学）穗；穗状花序

3. th' = the

4. between：*Adverb* in or along the space separating two objects or regions 夹在两物（或两个区域）之间的空间中（e.g. layers of paper with tar in between 两层之间有焦油的一叠纸）

5. hurst：*Noun* a sandbank in the sea or a river（海或河中）沙洲；沙岸

6. foam：*Noun*［mass noun］a mass of small bubbles formed on or in liquid, typically by agitation or fermentation 泡沫

7. veil：*Verb*［with obj.］cover with or as though with a veil（似）以面纱遮掩

077 ::

送郭司仓　□王昌龄

映门淮水绿，留骑主人心。

明月随良掾，春潮夜夜深。

五绝原诗注释（Annotations to the Original Chinese Version）

此诗为盛唐著名诗人王昌龄（约690～698—756）的一首五绝，诗题为《送郭司仓》。一个月明之夜，诗人送别好友，有感而发，情真意切。王昌龄是盛唐一位边塞诗人。郭司仓为诗人王昌龄一位郭姓朋友，官职为"司仓"。

首联出句"映门淮水绿"，交代了地点，模糊了时间，引出首联对句"留骑主人心"。"骑"（jì），骑马的人；"留骑"，留住了骑马的人，就是留客之意。尾联："明月随良掾，春潮夜夜深"，主人的留客之心虽深如碧绿的淮水，却最终未能留住客人，即主人的好友郭司仓，那就愿明月伴着他一路前行，他是一个良掾——"良掾，指郭司仓。官署属员通称为'掾'，司仓为州郡长官之属员，故称'良掾'。"（李云

逸,1984:122)当然,这里的"良掾",还应该是好官、清官、廉官之意。

A Feeling from Seeing off Mr. Guo with Sicang as His Official Title

○By *WANG Chang-ling*

Reflective glow of Huaishui's green
Water forms on the door a scene,
Which makes me ask my guest to stay
For more drink ere he's on his way.
In vain, and let the bright moon go
With him, whose title's good but low.
But I remain alone in here,
List'ning to th' river's springtime tide
Rise higher each night loud and clear
As I think of him far and wide.

N. B.

1. *Sicang* is rather a low official title in ancient China, especially in Tang Dynasty. Here in this poem, the poet's friend Mr. Guo is such an official, who is expected to be a good and clean one.

2. *Huaihe* or *Huaishui* is the Huaihe River or Huaishui River for short, and in particular, Huaishui (River) is the name of the river in ancient China. Located in the eastern part of China and between the Yellow River and the Yangtze River, it is one of the seven biggest rivers in China, which rises in China's southern He'nan Province and flows 1,000 km (621 miles) generally eastwards mainly through He'nan, Anhui and Jiangsu provinces to empty into the Huanghai Sea (the Yellow Sea), one of the inner seas of China, and the Yangtze River. In addition, Huaishui exerts a great influence upon Chinese men of letters, and as an important literary image, it is often mentioned in classical Chinese poetry.

Annotations to Its Version of English Verse（韵体译诗注释）

1. title：*Noun* a name that describes someone's position or job 职称；职务（e.g. Leese assumed the title of director-general. 利斯担任局长职务。）

2. reflective：*Adjective* produced by reflection 反射产生的（e.g. a colourful reflective glow 色彩绚丽的反射光）

3. glow：*Noun* [in sing.] a steady radiance of light or heat 发出光（或热）（e.g. The setting sun cast a deep red glow over the city. 落日给城市上空投下一道深红色的霞光。）

4. ere：*Preposition & Conjunction*（poetic/literary or archaic）before（in time）（诗/文用法或古旧用法）在……之前（在时间上）（e.g. We hope you will return ere long. 我们希望你很快回来。）

5. in vain：without success or a result 徒劳地（e.g. They waited in vain for a response. 他们白等回音。）

6. List'ning = Listening

7. th' = the

8. loud and clear：said in a very clear voice or expressed very clearly 响亮而清晰；清楚而明白（e.g. Tommy's voice came loud and clear from the back row. 汤米的声音从后排传来，响亮而清晰。）

9. far and wide：everywhere and many places；over a large area 到处；广泛地

078 ::

清溪泛舟　　□张旭

旅人倚征棹，薄暮起劳歌。
笑揽清溪月，清辉不厌多。

五绝原诗注释（Annotations to the Original Chinese Version）

张旭（675—约750）在五绝《清溪泛舟》中写出了诗人在清溪泛舟时的自由和洒脱，轻松与狂放，这也许是受船工"劳歌"的感染吧。首联中，"旅人"略显疲态而"倚征棹"，其中的"棹"原为划船的用具，在此应是用来借指船，而且船已经行得很远了。接近傍晚时，有的船工唱起了船歌。尾联中，也许受船歌感染，诗人欲捞起清溪中的月影，甚至还想尽量多拥有明月的辉光。

A Boat Trip through the Limpid Stream
○By *ZHANG Xu*

I travel far in a boat small,

Against whose edge I tiredly loll,

And near to dusk shanties I hear,

Which pour into me lots of cheer.

Then with a smile I try to fish

Th' moon out of th' clear stream as I wish,

And to collect its light as much

As both my longing hands can touch.

Annotations to Its Version of English Verse（韵体译诗注释）

1. limpid：*Adjective*（of a liquid）free of anything that darkens；completely clear（液体）清澈的；明净的

2. loll：*Verb* [no obj., with adverbial] sit, lie, or stand in a lazy, relaxed way 懒洋洋地坐（或躺、站）（e. g. The two girls lolled in their chairs. 两个女孩懒洋洋地坐在椅子上。）

3. shanty：*Noun*（also chanty or sea shanty）（pl. shanties）a song with alternating solo and chorus, of a kind originally sung by sailors while performing physical labour together 水手的劳动号子

4. cheer：*Noun*（also good cheer）[mass noun] cheerfulness, optimism, or confidence 快乐；乐观；信心（e. g. an attempt to inject a little cheer into this gloomy season 试着为这阴郁的季节里注入点快乐）

5. fish：*Verb* [with obj.]（fish something out）pull or take something out of water or a container or receptacle 把……拖出水面（或容器）；打捞出（e. g. The body of a woman had been fished out of the river. 从河里打捞出一具女尸。）

■ 079 ::

清夜酌　　□张说
秋阴士多感，雨息夜无尘。
清樽宜明月，复有平生人。

五绝原诗注释(Annotations to the Original Chinese Version)

张说(667—730)以日常生活中的场景起兴,转笔写"清樽宜明月",言清香的美酒适宜在明亮的月下畅饮,结句似乎对人生有所感悟——"复有平生人"。可以说,"人们难免多愁善感,但要学会搁置苦恼事,恢复平常心,让自己有张有弛。"(文东,2015:192)

Drinking Carefree at Moonlit Night

○By *ZHANG Yue*

In an autumnal gloomy day,
One tends to be distressed and grey
Until th' rain stops in th' eve, and th' sky
Is clear as crystal with th' moon high
Shining on th' earth, making it right
Drinking carefree at moonlit night,
Which helps a person to stay sane
And live a normal life again.

Annotations to Its Version of English Verse(韵体译诗注释)

1. carefree: *Adjective* free from anxiety or responsibility 无忧无虑的;快乐舒畅的;没有责任的

2. moonlit: *Adjective* lit by the moon 月光照耀下的

3. autumnal: *Adjective* of, characteristic of, or occurring in autumn 秋季的;秋季出现(或发生)的(e.g. rich autumnal colours 绚丽多彩的秋色)

4. gloomy: *Adjective* (gloomier, gloomiest) dark or poorly lit, especially so as to appear depressing or frightening 黑暗的;光线不好的(尤指看起来压抑或恐怖)(e.g. a gloomy corridor badly lit by oil lamps 用油灯照明的阴森森的走廊)

5. distressed: *Adjective* suffering from extreme anxiety, sorrow, or pain(极度)焦虑的;悲伤的;痛苦的(e.g. I was distressed at the news of his death. 听到他的死讯我非常难过。)

6. grey or gray: *Adjective* dull and nondescript; without interest or character 平淡无奇的;无明显特征的;单调乏味的(e.g. the grey daily routine 无聊的日常事务)

7. th' = the

8. eve：*Noun*（chiefly poetic/literary）evening(主要为诗/文用法)黄昏;傍晚

9. sane：*Adjective*（of a person）of sound mind; not mad or mentally ill（人）心智健全的;神志正常的;不疯的;无精神疾病的（e.g. Hard work kept me sane. 努力工作使我心智正常。）

080 ::

小院　□唐彦谦

小院无人夜,烟斜月转明。

清宵易惆怅,不必有离情。

五绝原诗注释（Annotations to the Original Chinese Version）

在《小院》一诗中,晚唐诗人唐彦谦(生卒年均不详)采用了类似王绩在《过酒家五首(其二)》(参见第065首)中"正话反说"的写法,含蓄表达了自己心中深深的惆怅之情和离别之意。具体说来,诗人以次句"烟斜月转明"来"掩盖离情,欲盖弥彰。接着索性强为辩解:清宵便易惆怅,何必要有离情"(文东,2015：105)。其实,小院无人之夜也就罢了,却偏偏烟雾斜散而去,令月无端转明,这已经燃起了诗人心中的惆怅和离情了。

In the Small Yard during the Night

○By *TANG Yan-qian*

No one keeps me company when

Fog smoky tilts sideways, and then

The moon dim turns gradually bright,

Shining on me and th' yard at night.

Since one tends to feel sick at heart

On lonely nights, the moody part

Of me at th' present time, if so,

Can be counted as sadness though?

N. B. In both ancient and modern China, the moon, be it a bright one or a full one, will always provoke people into various thinking. The full moon in particular always arouses in persons a sense of reunion with their sweetheart, spouse or family.

Annotations to Its Version of English Verse(韵体译诗注释)

1. yard: *Noun* (chiefly Brit.) a piece of uncultivated ground adjoining a building, typically one enclosed by walls or other buildings(主要为英国用法)(尤指用墙等建筑物)围起的空地;院子;庭院

2. keep sb'company: spend time with sb so that they are not alone 与某人做伴;陪伴某人 (e.g. I've promised to keep my sister company while her husband is away. 我答应妹妹在她丈夫不在的时候陪她。)

3. smoky: *Adjective* like smoke in colour or appearance(颜色或外观)像烟(雾)的 (e.g. smoky eyes 烟灰色眼睛)

4. th' = the

5. be/feel sick at heart (formal): be very unhappy or disappointed 很难过;非常失望 (e.g. When I realized the accident was my fault, I felt sick at heart. 认识到这起事故是我的错,我觉得心情沉痛。)

6. moody: *Adjective* giving an impression of melancholy or mystery 郁郁寡欢的;神秘莫测的

7. spouse: *Noun* a husband or wife, considered in relation to their partner 配偶(指丈夫或妻子)

第十一章 哲思五绝

Chapter 11　About Philosophical Thinking

■ **081** ::

蝉　□虞世南
垂緌饮清露,流响出疏桐。
居高声自远,非是藉秋风。

五绝原诗注释（**Annotations to the Original Chinese Version**）

初唐时期虞世南(558—638)所作五绝《蝉》,托物言志,别具特色。全诗以蝉起兴,整首诗寓意深刻。古人将帽带打结后下垂的部分称为"緌"(ruí),而蝉头部伸出的触须与此类似,故诗人在此用"緌"指代蝉的触须,实质上是蝉用以吸食的口器。《礼记·檀弓》曰:"范则冠而蝉有緌。"孔颖达疏:"蝉,蜩也。緌,谓蝉蠓长在口下,似冠之緌也。"①古人受知识所限,认为蝉居高树而"饮清露",实质上是在吸食树叶中的汁液。"流响"谓发出声响,实则"状蝉声的长鸣不已"(霍松林,1991:12);"疏桐"可能指粗壮的(梧)桐树,可能指疏落的(梧)桐树,也可能指枝叶稀疏的(梧)桐树。另外,严格说来,桐树应为油桐树,但有时候也用来指代梧桐树。

---

① 转引自"霍松林,1991:12"。

The Cicada

○By *YU Shi-nan*

To suck dew crystal clear

It lowers its mouthparts up here

In th' phoenix tree, from whose

Sparse branches its nonstop songs ooze.

'Tis th' height that far away

Helps th' insect greatly to convey

Its songs, but not the air

In autumn that moves to spread th' blare.

Annotations to Its Version of English Verse (韵体译诗注释)

1. cicada: *Noun* a large bug with long transparent wings, occurring chiefly in warm countries. The male cicada makes a loud shrill droning noise after dark by vibrating two membranes on its abdomen 蝉

2. dew: *Noun* [mass noun] tiny drops of water that form on cool surfaces at night, when atmospheric vapour condenses 露;露滴;露水

3. mouthpart: *Noun* (usu. mouthparts) (Zoology) any of the appendages, typically found in pairs, surrounding the mouth of an insect or other arthropod and adapted for feeding (动物学)(昆虫或其他节肢动物的)口器

4. th' = the

5. phoenix tree: deciduous tree widely grown in southern United States as an ornamental for its handsome maplelike foliage and long racemes of yellow-green flowers followed by curious leaflike pods 梧桐树

6. non-stop or nonstop: *Adjective* continuing without stopping or pausing 无停顿的 (e.g. We had two days of almost non-stop rain. 我们这里连着下了两天的雨几乎没停过。)

7. ooze: *Verb* [no obj., with adverbial of direction] (of a fluid) slowly trickle or seep out of something; move in a slow, creeping way (液体)渗出;慢慢流出 (e.g. Blood was oozing from a wound in his scalp. 鲜血从他头上的伤口处慢慢渗出。)

8. 'Tis = It is

9. height: *Noun* the quality of being tall or high 高度 (e.g. Her height marked

her out from other women. 她在女人中身高出众。)

10. convey: *Verb* [with obj.] transport or carry to a place 载送;输送 (e. g. Pipes were laid to convey water to the house. 铺了水管,将水输送到住宅。)

11. blare: *Noun* (in sing.) a loud, harsh sound 响而刺耳的声音 (e. g. a blare of trumpets 刺耳的喇叭声)

082 ::

鸟鸣涧　□王维

人闲桂花落,夜静春山空。

月出惊山鸟,时鸣春涧中。

五绝原诗注释(**Annotations to the Original Chinese Version**)

唐玄宗开元(713—741)年间,诗人王维(701—761)游历江南,拜访了友人皇甫岳,对其所居的云溪别墅流连忘返并写下《皇甫岳云溪杂题五首》,而《鸟鸣涧》便是其中的第一首。此诗表现了夜晚春山的静谧之美(可与第049首参看),但却以动态的意象,如花落、月出、(鸟)鸣等作衬托,愈显春山之静谧。"涧"为山间流水的沟;"桂花"即木樨,品种不一,有的春天开花,有的秋花开花。诗中写的应该是春天开花的桂花。

The Ravine above Which a Bird's Chirp Rings

○By *WANG Wei*

A man who is not busy may

Sense th' flowers falling off the Sweet

Osmanthus in a carefree way

In th' vast of mountains high, discrete,

Where no individual is seen

And th' spring night is a tranquil scene.

A sudden look at th' rising moon

Makes a bird panic-stricken soon.

Its chirp at times rings 'bove th' ravine

Whereas its shape remains unseen.

Annotations to Its Version of English Verse（韵体译诗注释）

1. chirp：*Verb*（no obj.）(typically of a small bird or an insect) utter a short, sharp, high-pitched sound(尤指小鸟或昆虫)吱吱叫；唧唧叫

2. ravine：*Noun* a deep, narrow gorge with steep sides 沟壑；皱谷；冲沟

3. th' = the

4. Sweet Osmanthus：It is a species native to Asia from the Himalayas through southern China (Guizhou, Sichuan, Yunnan) to Taiwan and southern Japan and southeast Asia as far south as Cambodia and Thailand 桂花；木樨

5. carefree：*Adjective* free from anxiety or responsibility 无忧无虑的；快乐舒畅的；没有责任的

6. vast：*Noun*（usu. the/a vast）(chiefly poetic) immense or boundless space (主要为诗歌用法)茫茫；无边无际的空间

7. discrete：*Adjective* individually separate and distinct 分离的；分立的；个别的

8. tranquil：*Adjective* free from disturbance；calm 平静的；镇静的

9. panic-stricken：(also panic-struck) *Adjective* affected with panic; very frightened 惊慌失措的；惊恐万分的（e.g. The panic-stricken victims rushed out of their blazing homes. 惊恐万状的受害者们从烈焰腾腾的家中拼命往外跑。）

10. chirp：*Noun* a short, sharp, high-pitched sound 吱吱声；唧唧声

11. at times：sometimes; on occasions 有时；间或

12. 'bove = above

083 ::

溪口云　□张文姬

溶溶溪口云，才向溪中吐。
不复归溪中，还作溪中雨。

五绝原诗注释（Annotations to the Original Chinese Version）

张文姬(生卒年均不详)为"鲍参军妻"（刘永济，1981：388），《全唐诗》存其诗共四首。张文姬是一位诗人，一位观察力极强的诗人。在她生活的那个时代，她就敏锐地注意到大自然中水是循环往复的：溪水蒸发，变成天上的云彩；云降甘霖，最终落入溪流之中。如果说诗人张文姬有所表达的话，可能是想表达她对丈夫忠贞不渝的

爱情吧。当然,诗无达诂,读诗的人不同,对诗的理解也不尽相同。首句中,"溶溶"为宽广之意,引申为明净、洁白的样子。

The Cloud above the Stream

○By ZHANG Wen-ji

Above the stream rising in flight,

The cloud, which is clean, wide and white,

Fills it up by turning to rain,

While going back appears in vain.

Annotations to Its Version of English Verse（韵体译诗注释）

1. stream：*Noun* a small, narrow river 小河;小溪

2. flight：*Noun* [mass noun] the action or process of flying through the air 飞行;飞翔（e.g. an eagle in flight 飞翔中的鹰）

3. in vain：without success or a result 徒劳地（e.g. They waited in vain for a response. 他们白等回音。）

084 ::

小松　　□王建

小松初数尺,未有直生枝。

闲即傍边立,看多长却迟。

五绝原诗注释（Annotations to the Original Chinese Version）

在《小松》这首诗中,王建(768—835)以小小的松树起兴,似乎要说明一定的道理。诗人希望小松快快长大,于是没事儿就站立在小松旁边,但似乎没有什么效果,那小松反而"看多长却迟"——急于求成,反而不成,还须脚踏实地,顺其自然。另外,汉语中的"尺",一般而言一米等于三尺,一尺相当于 33.33 厘米。英文中的"尺",即"英尺"(foot),一英尺等于十二英寸,一英尺相当于 30.48 厘米。所以,在翻译中可以采用归化法,化"尺"为"英尺"。

A Pine-tree Sapling

○By *WANG Jian*

Without a bough at its young stage,

It stands just a few feet to gauge.
And then whenever I'm free,
I will be standing by the tree—
The more on it I fix my eyes,
The slower it grows in its size.

Annotations to Its Version of English Verse(韵体译诗注释)

1. pine：*Noun*（also pine tree）an evergreen coniferous tree which has clusters of long needle-shaped leaves. Many kinds are grown for the soft timber, which is widely used for furniture and pulp, or for tar and turpentine 松树

2. sapling：*Noun* a young tree, especially one with a slender trunk（尤指树干细长的）幼树

3. bough：*Noun* a main branch of a tree 树枝；大树枝（e.g. apple boughs laden with blossom 开满了花的苹果树枝）

4. gauge：*Verb*［with obj.］estimate or determine the magnitude, amount, or volume of 估计（或判断）级别（数量或体积）（e. g. Astronomers can gauge the star's intrinsic brightness. 天文学家可以判断出星星的内在亮度。）

085 ::

放鱼　□李群玉

早觅为龙去，江湖莫漫游。
须知香饵下，触口是铦钩。

五绝原诗注释（Annotations to the Original Chinese Version）

从《放鱼》这一诗题来看，唐代诗人李群玉（808—862）似乎在诗体中写的是对所放之鱼的嘱托和告诫，富有哲理性。惠子曰："子非鱼，安知鱼之乐？"在鱼的世界里，鱼活着的最高境界似乎是成龙。譬如鲤鱼跳龙门的传说，譬如《艺文类聚》卷九六辛氏《三秦记》："河津一名龙门，大鱼积龙门数千不得上，上者为龙。"①所以在首联中，诗人嘱托自己所放生之鱼早日成龙，莫贪恋江湖，因江湖危机四伏，转而

---

① 转引自"霍松林，1991：873-874"。

告诫所放生之鱼:"须知香饵下,触口是铦钩。"结句中的"铦(xiān)钩",指的是锋利的鱼钩。所谓成龙,可以说是"到一个广阔自由没有机心的地方,而到达之前,危机四伏,尤其要提防香饵包藏的利钩"(文东,2015:149)。

Advice to the Captive Fish Who Is to Be Set Free

○By *LI Qun-yu*

Pursue your dream with no delay

To th' river long and th' lake far wide,

But in the waters don't stray,

Where there's life risk to hide—

The tasty food enticing you

Contains a deadly sharp hook, too.

Annotations to Its Version of English Verse(韵体译诗注释)

1. captive: *Adjective* imprisoned or confined 被关押的;被囚禁的(e.g. a captive animal 一只被捕获的动物)

2. pursue: *Verb* seek to attain or accomplish (a goal), especially over a long period 追求;寻求(e.g. Should people pursue their own happiness at the expense of others? 人们是否可以以牺牲他人的幸福为代价来追求自己的幸福?)

3. th' = the

4. water: (waters) the water of a particular sea, river, or lake 水域(e.g. the waters of Hudson Bay 哈得逊湾水域)

5. stray: *Verb* [no obj., with adverbial of direction] (poetic/literary) wander or roam in a specified direction (诗/文用法)漫步;徘徊;游荡(e.g. Over these mounds the Kurdish shepherd strays. 库尔德牧羊人游荡在这些土岗上。)

6. risk: *Noun* [with modifier] a thing regarded as likely to result in a specified danger 具有危害性的事物(e.g. Gloss paint can burn strongly and pose a fire risk. 有光涂料易猛烈燃烧,有引起火灾的危险。)

7. entice: *Verb* [with obj.] attract or tempt by offering pleasure or advantage 诱使;诱惑(e.g. a show which should entice a new audience into the theatre 一部会吸引一批新观众观看的影片)

8. deadly: *Adverb* extremely 极度地;极其(e.g. a deadly serious remark 极其

严肃的话）

9. hook：*Noun*（also fish-hook）a bent piece of metal, typically barbed and baited, for catching fish 鱼钩（多指带刺和鱼饵的）

086 ::

幽居乐　□施肩吾
万籁不在耳，寂寥心境清。
无妨数茎竹，时有萧萧声。

五绝原诗注释（Annotations to the Original Chinese Version）
诗人施肩吾(780—861)在幽居期间，心静如止水，不受任何外界之物的影响，"从而领悟到若内心真正宁静，外界影响便将无能为力。"（文东，2015：208）"籁"原指孔穴里发出的声音，后用来泛指声响、声音。幽居中的诗人自得其乐，万籁皆不入耳，寂寥之时仍内心清净，就算是数根竹子时而被萧萧的风吹得发出嘈杂的声响也无妨，幽居之乐依旧。

My Single-minded Leisure to Live in Seclusion
○By *SHI Jian-wu*

In my single-mindedness state,
No sounds of any kind will bait
My ears; in my boredom, my mind
Remains at peace, not in a bind—
Bamboos make noise time and again,
Failing to make my nervous strain.

Annotations to Its Version of English Verse（韵体译诗注释）

1. single-minded：*Adjective* having or concentrating on only one aim or purpose 一心一意；专心致志的（e.g. the single-minded pursuit of profit 一味追求利润）

2. seclusion：*Noun* [mass noun] the state of being private and away from other people 隔绝；隐居（e.g. They enjoyed ten days of peace and seclusion. 他们享受了十天与世隔绝的宁静生活。）

3. bait：*Verb* deliberately annoy or taunt (someone) 骚扰；逗弄（e.g. The oth-

er boys revelled in baiting him about his love of literature. 其他男孩都爱拿他对文学的热爱来嘲弄他。)

4. boredom: *Noun* [mass noun] the state of feeling bored 厌烦;厌倦;无聊(e. g. I'll die of boredom if I live that long. 活那么久,我会无聊死的。)

5. be at peace: be calm or quiet 镇定;平静(e. g. He's much more at peace with himself now than he used to be. 现在他比以前心平气和多了。)

6. bind: *Noun* a problematical situation 困境;尴尬的处境(e. g. He is in a political bind over the abortion issue. 堕胎问题使他在政治上陷入了困境。)

7. bamboo: *Noun* [mass noun] a giant woody grass which grows chiefly in the tropics, where it is widely cultivated 竹;竹子

8. noise: *Noun* [mass noun] a series or combination of loud, confused sounds, especially when causing disturbance 嘈杂声;噪音(e. g. vibration and noise from traffic 来往车辆发出的震动和嘈杂声)

9. strain: *Noun* [mass noun] a state of tension or exhaustion resulting from a severe or excessive demand on the strength, resources, or abilities of someone or something 极度紧张;过度劳累(e. g. the telltale signs of nervous strain 神经过度紧张的明显迹象)

087 ::

退居漫题七首(其七) □司空图

燕拙营巢苦,鱼贪触网惊。

岂缘身外事,亦似我劳形。

五绝原诗注释(Annotations to the Original Chinese Version)

唐代诗人司空图(837—908)归隐后所作《退居漫题七首》,是一组五言绝句,描述了诗人看似平静舒闲实则内心起伏的"林塘"生活。在《退居漫题七首(其七)》中,诗人以燕、鱼起兴,转笔发出疑问:"岂缘身外事,亦似我劳形?"——难道燕、鱼因为身外之事,也跟我一样身体疲惫吗?燕、鱼劳形为生计,而人呢?劳形则可能为了名利。那样的话,不仅劳形,而且还会苦心。

Random Thoughts while Living in Seclusion (Seventh of Seven Poems with the Same Title)

○By *SIKONG Tu*

The swallow diligent takes pains
To build its nest, while th' greedy fish
Into net dives for food and strains
In fright to break free with a wish.
Do they do such things in th' same way
As I do every single day
To make a living but to tire
Me out for things to which I 'spire?

Annotations to Its Version of English Verse(韵体译诗注释)

1. random: *Adjective* made, done, happening, or chosen without method or conscious decision 胡乱的;无一定规则的;任意;任意选取的

2. seclusion: *Noun* [mass noun] the state of being private and away from other people 隔绝;隐居(e.g. They enjoyed ten days of peace and seclusion. 他们享受了十天与世隔绝的宁静生活。)

3. swallow: *Noun* a migratory swift-flying songbird with a forked tail and long pointed wings, feeding on insects in flight 燕子

4. pain: *Noun* (pains) careful effort; great care or trouble 辛苦;努力;苦心;操心(e.g. She took pains to see that everyone ate well. 她煞费苦心确保每个人都吃得好。)

5. th' = the

6. strain: *Verb* [no obj.] make a strenuous and continuous effort 尽力;努力;使劲(e.g. His voice was so quiet that I had to strain to hear it. 他的声音那么轻,我得使劲听才听得见。)

7. tire: *Verb* [with obj.] cause to feel in need of rest or sleep; weary 使感到疲劳(或累)(e.g. The training tired us out. 训练把我们累坏了。)

8. 'spire = aspire

9. aspire: *Verb* [no obj.] direct one's hopes or ambitions towards achieving something 渴望;有志于(e.g. We never thought that we might aspire to those heights. 我们从来没有想到自己会渴望达到那些高度。)

第十二章 悲秋五绝

Chapter 12 About Autumnal Unpleasantness

■ **088** ::

汾上惊秋　　□苏颋
北风吹白云,万里渡河汾。
心绪逢摇落,秋声不可闻。

五绝原诗注释(**Annotations to the Original Chinese Version**)
苏颋(670—727)在《汾上惊秋》中抒发了自己复杂的情感。诗人在开元十一年(公元723年)冬,被外放为益州大都督长史,直到开元十三年(公元725年)才调回长安。其间逢秋,诗人写下此诗。诗题中,"汾"指汾河,是黄河的第二大支流,"源出山西武宁县管岑山,在河津县入黄河"(霍松林,1991:91),但与最新的地理考查结果有所不同。首联基本上化用了汉武帝刘彻《秋风辞》中的两句:"秋风起兮白云飞"以及"泛楼船兮济汾河"。次句中,"河汾"是黄河与汾河的合称,指"黄河和汾河相交汇之处"(霍松林,1991:91)。尾联中,"摇落"或许是化用了宋玉《九辩》中的两句:"悲哉秋之为气也,萧瑟兮草木摇落而变衰。"诗人苏颋心绪不佳,偏又见草木逢秋凋零,自然就"秋声不可闻"了:秋天的风瑟瑟地吹,诗人再也不想听到了。

A Surprise Sight of Autumnal View along the Fenshui River
○By *SU Ting*

The north wind chilly blows away
A cloud white, which is in a way
Like me, who crosses th' water where
The tributary joins the one
Which's larger and far, far to run,
And th' sight of falling leaves through th' air
Makes me feel sad and hate to hear
The wind 'loud wailing far and near.

N. B. Fenshui River (Today's Fenhe River) in ancient China, which rises in a mountainous area of Shanxi Province and flows generally southwest before entering the Yellow River in the province, thus forming its second largest tributary, flows through six cities of the province, and it used to be a symbol like holy land for all men of letters, who feel it a great honor to mention it in their poetry.

Annotations to Its Version of English Verse (韵体译诗注释)

1. autumnal: *Adjective* of, characteristic of, or occurring in autumn 秋季的;秋季出现(或发生)的 (e.g. rich autumnal colours 绚丽多彩的秋色)

2. chilly: *Adjective* (chillier, chilliest) uncomfortably or unpleasantly cold 寒冷的

3. th' = the

4. tributary: *Noun* (pl. tributaries) a river or stream flowing into a larger river or lake (河川或湖泊的)支流 (e.g. the Illinois River, a tributary of the Mississippi 伊利诺斯河,密西西比河支流)

5. which's = which is

6. 'loud = aloud

7. wail: *Verb* make a sound resembling a cry of pain, grief, or anger 呼啸;悲鸣 (e.g. The wind wailed and buffeted the timber structure. 狂风呼啸,吹打着那幢木结构的建筑物。)

第十二章　悲秋五绝

■ **089** ∷

秋日　□耿湋

反照入闾巷，忧来与谁语。

古道无人行，秋风动禾黍。

五绝原诗注释（**Annotations to the Original Chinese Version**）

耿湋（生卒年均不详）是宝应元年（公元762年）进士。在《秋日》一诗中，他描写了古道上秋日黄昏的凄凉景象：曾经繁华的古道如今一派荒凉，但两旁禾黍（禾与黍的合称，泛指粮食作物）依旧生长，随着秋风摇摆。首句"反照"，一作"返照"，指"夕阳反射的余晖"（李霁野，2016：141）；"闾（lǘ）巷"指里巷、邻里。次句"忧来与谁语"，一作"愁来谁共语"，义为"心里惆怅谁人可以共语？"（文东，2015：56）。尾联出句中"无人行"，一作"少人行"，尾联"有伤时的感慨，因为战乱使唐王朝盛世成为过去了"（李霁野，2016：141）。

On an Autumn Day

○By *GENG Wei*

Reflective glow lights th' alley where

I stay and at the glow I stare,

Which causes me to feel distressed;

And whom should I confide in best?

Before me lies the ancient road,

Along which people often strode,

But now on it none is in sight,

Except the crops on either side

Of it, which stand in farmland wide

While autumn winds blow day and night.

Annotations to Its Version of English Verse（韵体译诗注释）

1. reflective：*Adjective* produced by reflection 反射产生的（e.g. a colourful reflective glow 色彩绚丽的反射光）

2. glow：*Noun* (in sing.) a steady radiance of light or heat 发出光（或热）（e.

g. The setting sun cast a deep red glow over the city. 落日给城市上空投下一道深红色的霞光。)

3. th' = the

4. alley：*Noun* a narrow passageway between or behind buildings（房屋之间或后面的狭窄）小巷；通道

5. distressed：*Adjective* suffering from extreme anxiety, sorrow, or pain（极度）焦虑的；悲伤的；痛苦的（e.g. I was distressed at the news of his death. 听到他的死讯我非常难过。)

6. confide：*Verb*（no obj.）(confide in) trust (someone) enough to tell them of such a secret or private matter 因信任(某人)而向其吐露(秘密或私事)

7. farmland：*Noun* [mass noun]（also farmlands) land used for farming 农田；耕地

■ 090 ::

伤秋　□钱起
岁去人头白,秋来树叶黄。
搔头向黄叶,与尔共悲伤。

五绝原诗注释（Annotations to the Original Chinese Version）

在五绝《伤秋》中,钱起(生卒年均不详,公元751年前后在世)采用了拟人化的手法,赋予黄树叶以生命,人与树(确切来说,与黄树叶)似乎"成了知音,感情上也产生了共鸣,可以相互交谈,共话悲伤"(文东,2015：146)。此诗首联入对,但首句不入韵。尾联中,"搔"意为挠,指用手指甲轻刮。另外,此诗系钱起《蓝田溪杂咏二十二首》中的一首,这二十二首诗每一首都自带题目。

The Autumnal Sadness

○By *QIAN Qi*

With th' passage of time I have more
Hair grey at present than before,
And similarly, yellow grow
More tree leaves when autumn winds blow.
And so, I scratch my head and say

To one of them, "You and I may
Share mutual feelings, and for now,
We both feel sad, you should avow."

Annotations to Its Version of English Verse(韵体译诗注释)

1. autumnal: *Adjective* of, characteristic of, or occurring in autumn 秋季的;秋季出现(或发生)的(e.g. rich autumnal colours 绚丽多彩的秋色)

2. th' = the

3. passage: *Noun* the act or process of moving forward 经过;消逝(e.g. Despite the passage of time she still loved him. 尽管时光流逝,她依然爱他。)

4. scratch: *Verb* rub (a part of one's body) with one's fingernails to relieve itching 挠;搔痒

5. avow: *Verb* [reporting verb] assert or confess openly 宣称;供认;公开承认(e.g. He avowed that he had voted Labour in every election. 他坦然承认每届大选他都投工党一票。)

■ 091 ::

立秋前一日览镜　　□李益
万事销身外,生涯在镜中。
惟将满鬓雪,明日对秋风。

五绝原诗注释(Annotations to the Original Chinese Version)

李益(748—829)在《立秋前一日览镜》中传达出人生不如意之时的悲秋意味。诗题中,"览镜"含有以镜为鉴之意,看到镜中无望的自己,已经是满鬓霜雪,却仍要面对明日的瑟瑟秋风,仍对无望的自己和明天抱有一线希望。尽管"镜中容貌的变衰反映了生命的流驰"(霍松林,1991:446),但以立秋之日为临界点,过去的就让它过去,"满鬓雪"的自己明日立秋后依然会有所准备,有所期望,期望有奇迹发生而改变人生。这就是封建时代大多数文人的心态:惟将满鬓雪,明日对秋风。

Thoughts while Looking in the Mirror One Day before the Beginning of Autumn

○By *LI Yi*

All bygones are forever gone,
No matter how they make me wan;
My past deed's like th' image of me,
Which stills in th' mirror, great or wee.
Though for now, I have more hair grey,
I cherish yet a dream today
That after th' morrow I'll still brave
Bleak autumn winds with hope to crave.

Annotations to Its Version of English Verse（韵体译诗注释）

1. bygone：*Noun* noun（usu. bygones）a thing dating from an earlier time 过去的事情

2. wan：*Adjective*（of a person's complexion or appearance）pale and giving the impression of illness or exhaustion（人的脸色或外表）苍白的；病态的；疲倦的（e. g. She was looking wan and bleary-eyed. 她看上去脸色苍白，睡眼惺忪。）

3. th' = the

4. image：*Noun* an optical appearance or counterpart produced by light or other radiation from an object reflected in a mirror or refracted through a lens 镜像

5. still：*Verb* make or become still；quieten（使）平静；（使）寂静；（使）静止；止住（e. g. The din in the hall stilled. 大厅里的喧闹停了下来。）

6. wee：*Adjective*（weer, west）（chiefly Scottish）little（主要为苏格兰用法）很少的；微小的（e. g. when I was just a wee bairn 当我还是小孩时）

7. cherish：*Verb* keep in one's mind（a hope or ambition）抱有；怀有（希望或野心）（e. g. He had long cherished a secret fantasy about his future. 他一直对自己的未来抱有秘不告人的幻想。）

8. morrow：*Noun*（the morrow）（archaic or poetic/literary）the following day（古旧用法或诗/文用法）翌日（e. g. On the morrow they attacked the city. 次日，他们进攻了城市。）

9. brave：*Verb*（with obj.）endure or face（unpleasant conditions or behaviour）

without showing fear 勇敢面对（e. g. He pulled on his coat ready to brave the elements. 他穿好大衣准备面对恶劣的天气。）

10. crave：Verb（with obj.）feel a powerful desire for（something）渴望；热望（e. g. If only she had shown her daughter the love she craved. 要是她向女儿表示过她所渴望的爱就好了。）

092 ::

蜀道后期　□张说
客心争日月，来往预期程。
秋风不相待，先至洛阳城。

五绝原诗注释（Annotations to the Original Chinese Version）

唐朝大臣兼诗人张说（667—730）在《蜀道后期》一诗中，以独特的视角写出了秋来欲归却无法及时归的急切心情。诗题中，借"蜀道"代蜀地，用以指代诗人外出任职的四川一带，"后期"则指诗人未能按照预期的行程归家，含有将自己预定的归期推后之意。沈德潜在《唐诗别裁》中如此评说："以秋风先到，形出己之后期，巧心潜发。"①首联已经表现出诗人思归的急切心情：客居他乡，争分夺秒，就连归期也预计妥当了（当然，在这之前，到来的日期也许有所预计，或者说，归去后再回来的日期也有所预计）。但是，事与愿违，由于某些原因诗人无法预期返回。尾联中，诗人笔锋一转，转而埋怨秋风不等自己，先到了自己的思归之处——洛阳城。尽管诗人采用了巧妙而独特的视角，尾联实质上是说诗人无法按期返回，或者换个角度说，还没等诗人返回，萧瑟的秋天就已经到来。尾联中，诗人将秋风拟人化，委婉表达了自己悲秋的情怀。

My Late Return to Luoyang City, My Hometown, from the Region of Shu

○By *ZHANG Yue*

Far, far away from home when I'm,

---

① 转引自"霍松林，1991：112"。

In working hard I lose no time,
And even pre-arrange when to
Return and bid them all adieu.
But contrary to my pre-thought,
The autum wind awaits me not,
And blows its way nonstop ahead
Of me to my hometown instead.

N. B. The Region of Shu and Luoyang City: The Region of Shu ("Shudi" in Chinese), where the poet Zhang Yue temporarily works, is approximately today's Sichuan Province. Luoyang City (Approximately today's Luoyang City, He'nan Province), the hometown of the poet, is the capital of Wuzhou Dynasty—the Tang Dynasty under the reign of Empress Wu Ze-tian. But mostly as the eastern capital of Tang Dynasty and capitals of thirteen dynasties or kingdoms in the long Chinese history, it used to be a second holy land for all men of letters, the first one being Chang'an. Especially in Tang Dynasty, Luoyang has also become a dream place of poets, who feel it a great honor to go to that place and often mention it in their poetry.

Annotations to Its Version of English Verse（韵体译诗注释）

1. to lose/waste no time (in doing sth): to do sth quickly and without delay 毫不拖延地（做某事）；不浪费时间；迅速行动：(e.g. As soon as she arrived back home, she lost no time in visiting all her old friends. 她一回到家乡就立刻去拜访所有的老朋友。)

2. adieu: *Noun* (pl. adieus or adieux) a goodbye 再见 (e.g. They bade us all adieu. 他们向我们大家说再见。)

3. await: *Verb* (of an event or circumstance) be in store for (someone) (事件或情况) 等着（某人）(e.g. Many dangers await them. 种种危险在等待着他们。)

4. non-stop or nonstop: *Adverb* without stopping or pausing 不休息地；不断地

5. holy land: *Noun* [as noun a holy land] a place which attracts people of a particular group or with a particular interest 圣地 (e.g. Holland is a holy land for jazz enthusiasts. 荷兰是爵士乐狂热者的圣地。)

第十二章　悲秋五绝

093 ::

玉台体十二首（其九）　□权德舆

秋风一夜至，吹尽后庭花。

莫作经时别，西邻是宋家。

五绝原诗注释（Annotations to the Original Chinese Version）

　　这首诗为中唐诗人权德舆（759—818）的《玉台体》，此诗题下共有十二首，诗体为"秋风一夜至，吹尽后庭花。莫作经时别，西邻是宋家"的这一首，是其中的第九首。结句"西邻是宋家"中的"宋家"，指的是战国时期辞赋家宋玉的家。宋玉在历史上号称"美男子"，其本身也是一位才华横溢之人。有一次，为了答楚王之问，宋玉以"东邻美女"为例，硬是让楚王相信，登徒子才是"好色之徒"。其中，宋玉极尽溢美之词对东邻之女赞不绝口：

　　　　增之一分则太长，减之一分则太短；著粉则太白，施朱则太赤。眉如翠羽，肌如白雪，腰如素束，齿如含贝。嫣然一笑，惑阳城，迷下蔡。（宋玉《登徒子好色赋》）

　　此诗尾联中，诗人权德舆以一位女子的视角，用戏谑的口吻，反其意而用之，乖嗔地告诫出门在外的夫君："你离开我的时间可不要太长呀，要知道咱家的西邻可是'宋家'啊！"言外之意是说，西邻住的可是位美男子，但不乏"郎才"；含却未表之意则可能是说，"我"可是西邻的"东邻美女"啊，可谓"女貌"。西邻、东邻合在一起则是"郎才女貌"了。

Yutai-style Love Poetry（Ninth of Twelve Poems with the Same Title）

○By *QUAN De-yu*

The autumn wind overnight arrives—

Ah, backyard blossoms! None survives.

"One more year has passed since you leave.

How time flies, which makes me quite grieve!"

She thinks aloud, "Too long to stay

Away from home, it is no way!
Our western neighbor is a man
Of handsome features, who I can
Be sure looks like Song Yu, although
He is a man long time ago!"

N. B.

1. "*Yutai* Style" is a kind of poetic style usually adopted by ancient Chinese poets to describe love affairs especially from the perspective of a lady. In both ancient and modern China, the moon, be it a bright one or a full one, will always provoke people into various thinking. The full moon in particular always arouses in persons a sense of reunion with their sweetheart, spouse or family.

2. Song Yu is a literary man living in the ending of ancient China's Spring and Autumn and Warring States Period (770—221 bc), who is a man of handsome features and is also well-known for his literary talent. He once claimed that his western neighbor was a girl who was as fair as Helen. In view of the above, the lady in the poem implies in a way that she is also as fair as Helen for she is the very western neighbor, half-jokingly reminding her husband that he should be alert to his long absence from home.

Annotations to Its Version of English Verse（韵体译诗注释）

1. overnight: *Adverb* very quickly; suddenly 一夜之间

2. ah: *Exclamation* used to express a range of emotions including surprise, pleasure, sympathy, and realization 啊；呀（用于表示惊讶、喜悦、同情和意识到等一系列情绪）

3. backyard: *Noun* (Brit.) a yard at the back of a house or other building（英国用法）后院

4. blossom: *Noun* a flower or a mass of flowers, especially on a tree or bush（尤指树上的）花朵；花簇（e.g. The slopes were ablaze with almond blossom. 山坡上盛开着扁桃树花。）

5. grieve: *Verb* [no obj.] suffer grief 感到悲痛；伤心

6. think aloud: express one's thoughts as soon as they occur 自言自语，边想边说出声

7. no way: (informal) definitely not; never（非正式用法）不可能；决不；没门

儿(e.g. Are you going to stay at school after you're 16? – No way. I want to get a job. 满16岁后,你还会上学吗?——决不,我想找份工作。)

8. feature: *Noun* (usu. features) a part of the face, such as the mouth or eyes, making a significant contribution to its overall appearance 五官;容貌;长相

9. alert: *Adjective* quick to notice any unusual and potentially dangerous or difficult circumstances; vigilant 警惕的;警觉的;机警的

094 ::

中秋 □司空图

闲吟秋景外,万事觉悠悠。

此夜若无月,一年虚过秋。

五绝原诗注释（Annotations to the Original Chinese Version）

唐代诗人司空图(837—908)在五绝《中秋》中"可能借明月说事,比拟[sic]无明主则一生虚度"(文东,2015:222)。秋季闲吟秋景,这是再自然不过之事,也是人生乐事。除此之外,一切都是那么遥远,让诗人感觉忧郁,也许还心生不安。闲吟秋景,当然离不开秋月,特别是中秋夜的一轮明月。但是,中秋夜若是没有明月出现,那么这一年中的这个秋季算是白过了。整个秋季白过了,这一年也就等于白过了。另外,个别版本中,首联对句也写作"万事空悠悠"。

On the Mid-autumn Night

○By *SIKONG Tu*

I feel that all makes me depressed

Except taking delight with zest

In th' autumn view, which's writt'n in rhyme

Whenever I have some spare time.

However, on this very night,

If there in th' sky hangs no moon bright,

Then th' season autumn is spent in vain,

And th' whole year, with nothing to gain.

Annotations to Its Version of English Verse（韵体译诗注释）

1. depressed: *Adjective* (of a person) in a state of general unhappiness or de-

spondency（人）沮丧的；消沉的

2. zest：*Noun* [mass noun] great enthusiasm and energy 兴趣；兴味；热情（e. g. They campaigned with zest and intelligence. 他们带着热情与才智投身运动。）

3. th' = the

4. view：*Count. Noun* a sight or prospect, typically of attractive natural scenery, that can be taken in by the eye from a particular place 景色；美景（e.g. a fine view of the castle 城堡的美景）

5. which's = which is

6. writt'n = written

7. rhyme：*Noun* poetry or verse marked by such correspondence of sound 押韵诗；韵文（e.g. The clues were written in rhyme. 字谜线索是以韵诗形式写成的。）

8. in vain：without success or a result 徒劳地（e.g. They waited in vain for a response. 他们白等回音。）

第十三章 边塞五绝

Chapter 13 About Frontier Warfare

■ 095 ::

和张仆射塞下曲六首(其三)　　□卢纶
月黑雁飞高,单于夜遁逃。
欲将轻骑逐,大雪满弓刀。

五绝原诗注释(Annotations to the Original Chinese Version)

　　五绝《和张仆射塞下曲》(一作《塞下曲》)共有六首,诗体为"月黑雁飞高,单于夜遁逃。欲将轻骑逐,大雪满弓刀"的这一首,是其中的第三首。在《全唐诗》第 239 卷中,此诗诗题作《和张仆射塞下曲(一作卢纶诗)》,署名为钱起(生卒年均不详,公元 751 年前后在世),但在《全唐诗》第 278 卷中,此诗诗题作《和张仆射塞下曲》,署名则为卢纶(公元 739—799 年)。本书从之,视其为卢纶的作品。诗题中,"仆射"(pú yè)是中国秦至宋代的官名,大致为诸官之长,宋代以后被废除。"塞下曲"为乐府旧题,多写边塞军旅生活,算是古时候的一种战歌。

　　原诗首联"月黑雁飞高,单于夜遁逃"中的两句之间其实是有一定关联的,"雁飞高"是由"夜遁逃"引发的,是"夜遁逃"的征兆或结果。这样的逻辑关系,汉语思维理解起来问题不大,但译成英语则需通过修辞性调整,增加相关的逻辑关联词予以体现,或者调整前后顺序,令译诗更为符合英文的表达规范。其中,"单于"(chán yú)为匈奴的首领,是"匈奴君长之称"(霍松林,1991:451),诗中用以指代边塞入侵者的最高统帅。尾联中,"将"(jiāng)意为率领、带领;"弓刀",一解为如弓般弯曲的刀,一解为弓和刀的合称。尾联的翻译要把握住一个"欲"字,刻画的是出发追逐单于残部之前的情形,彰显的是军威和气势。

Poetry by Imitating Rhyming Style of "Ode to Frontier Warfare" by Mr. Zhang, General Manager of Officials (Third of Six Poems with the Same Title)

○By *LU Lun*

English Verse (1)

Chanyu, head of nomadic troop,

Escapes together with his group

On th' moonless night, which with a start

Makes some geese wild to th' sky high dart.

Light cavalry men are to chase

Their enemy for any trace,

With heavy snow adhering to

All their bow-shaped cold knives like glue.

English Verse (2)

Chanyu, head of nomadic troop,

Escapes together with his group

On th' moonless night, which with a start

Makes some geese wild to th' sky high dart.

Light cavalry men are to chase

Their enemy for any trace,

With heavy snow adhering to

All their bows and cold knives like glue.

Annotations to Its Version of English Verse（韵体译诗注释）

1. ode: *Noun* a classical poem of a kind originally meant to be sung 颂诗；赋

2. frontier: *Noun* a line or border separating two countries 边境；边界

3. warfare: *Noun* [mass noun] engagement in or the activities involved in war or conflict 战争；作战；斗争

4. verse: *Noun* [mass noun] writing arranged with a metrical rhythm, typically having a rhyme 诗；韵文；诗句

5. nomadic: *Adjective* relating to or characteristic of nomads 游牧的；流浪的

6. th' = the

7. start: *Noun* a sudden movement of surprise or alarm 惊跳；惊起（e. g. She awoke with a start. 她猛然惊醒。）

8. goose: *Noun* (pl. geese) a large waterbird with a long neck, short legs, webbed feet, and a short broad bill. Generally geese are larger than ducks and have longer necks and shorter bills 鹅

9. dart: *Verb* [no obj., with adverbial of direction] move or run somewhere suddenly or rapidly 急冲；飞奔；突然行进（e. g. She darted across the street. 她突然冲过马路。）

10. cavalry: *Noun* (pl. calvalries) [usu. treated as pl.] (historical) soldiers who fought on horseback（历史上的用法）骑兵

11. trace: *Noun or Mass Noun* a mark, object, or other indication of the existence or passing of something 痕迹；踪迹（e. g. The aircraft disappeared without trace. 飞机消失得无影无踪。）

12. adhere: *Verb* [no obj.] (adhere to) stick fast to (a surface or substance) 粘在(表面或物质)上（e. g. Paint won't adhere well to a greasy surface. 油腻的表面上，油漆粘不牢。）

13. bow: *Noun* a weapon for shooting arrows, typically made of a curved piece of wood joined at both ends by a taut string 弓

096 ::

塞下　□许浑

夜战桑干北，秦兵半不归。
朝来有乡信，犹自寄征衣。

五绝原诗注释（Annotations to the Original Chinese Version）

许浑（约791—约858）所作五绝《塞下》，实则为《塞下曲》的省称。如上节"095"中所注，"塞下曲"为乐府旧题，多写边塞军旅生活，算是古时候的一种战歌。

首句中，"桑干"，一作"桑乾（gān）"，指桑干河，"源出山西马邑县桑干山，东入河北及北京市郊外……古边塞征战之地。"（霍松林，1991：852）桑干河是塞北一条古老的河，孕育了两岸悠久的文化。次句中，"秦兵"指唐朝戍边军队，因唐朝都城位于关中，而关中又是秦朝旧地，故称唐军为秦兵。结句中，"征衣"，一作"寒衣"，指征战时穿的御寒衣服。尾联意同"白骨已枯沙上草，家人犹自寄寒衣"（沈彬《吊边人》），"诗言沙场雪满，深夜鏖兵，追侵晓归营，损折已近半数；而秦中少妇，犹预量寒意，远寄衣裘，不知梦里征人，已埋骨桑干河畔矣"（俞陛云，2011：153-154），可见战争之残酷与无情。

Ode to Frontier Warfare

○By *XU Hun*

The night sees one ferocious fight

In northern Sanggan River, where

Half th' men of Qin th' next morn lose sight

Of letters and coats warm to wear,

Which are sent from their home in spite

Of th' cruel fact that they may breathe ne'er.

N. B.

1. The Sanggan River, which rises in Sanggan Mountain of Shanxi Province, is an ancient river in the northern part of the Great Wall of China, where the frontier warfare was frequently waged against the invaders or for more land.

2. The "men of Qin" refers to the army men of Tang Dynasty (618—907), for Chang'an, its capital, lies in the region of the former Qin Dynasty (221—207 bc).

Annotations to Its Version of English Verse（韵体译诗注释）

1. ode：*Noun* a classical poem of a kind originally meant to be sung 颂诗；赋

2. frontier：*Noun* a line or border separating two countries 边境；边界

3. warfare：*Noun* [mass noun] engagement in or the activities involved in war or conflict 战争；作战；斗争

4. see：*Verb* be the time or setting of (something) 是……的时期（或背景）(e.g. The 1970s saw the beginning of a technological revolution. 20世纪70年代开始了一场技术革命。)

5. ferocious：*Adjective* savagely fierce, cruel, or violent 凶恶的；凶猛的；残忍的；狂暴的

6. th' = the

7. morn：*Noun* poetic/literary term for morning(诗/文用法)同"morning"

8. lose sight of：be no longer able to see 再也看不见

9. warm：*Adjective* (of clothes or coverings) made of a material that helps the body to retain heat; suitable for cold weather（衣服或遮盖物）保暖的；暖和的（e.g. a warm winter coat 暖和的冬衣）

10. ne'er = never

097 ::

闺怨词三首（其三） □白居易

关山征戍远，闺阁别离难。

苦战应憔悴，寒衣不要宽。

五绝原诗注释（Annotations to the Original Chinese Version）

白居易（772—846）所作《闺怨词》共计三首，诗体为"关山征戍远，闺阁别离难。苦战应憔悴，寒衣不要宽"的这一首，是其中的第三首。首句中，对"关山"的讨论可参看本书第二章"014"部分的注释。此诗首联交代背景：丈夫戍边，妇人经历着别离的痛苦，但却深切地牵挂着自己的丈夫，所以在尾联中，妇人"设想应为丈夫裁制不宽的寒衣，已在努力忍受自身痛苦，把丈夫需要放在首位"（文东，2015：166）。正是：

关山征戍，良人偏去得远，闺阁别离，妇人偏又觉得难。二语已尽情事，苦战应憔悴，寒衣不要宽，又十分体惜。忖量他因自己之难想到良人之苦。（徐增《说唐诗详解》）①

---

① 转引自"霍松林，1991：626—627"。

A Wife's Deep Concern for Her Husband Serving in the Frontier(Third of Three Poems with the Same Title)

○By *BAI Ju-yi*

For her, it's hard to sadly part
With him, her husband and sweetheart,
Who goes o'er th' mountain pass to fight
Wars on th' frontier far with no fright.
Fierce battles should leave him quite thin,
Which warns her that, should she begin
To sew a coat to show her care,
It'd be warm but not fat to wear.

Annotations to Its Version of English Verse（韵体译诗注释）

1. frontier：*Noun* a line or border separating two countries 边境；边界

2. o'er = over

3. th' = the

4. fight：*Verb* [with obj.] engage in (a war or battle) 打（仗）；参（战）(e.g. There was another war to fight. 还有一场仗要打。)

5. thin：*Adjective* (of a person) having little, or too little, flesh or fat on their body (人)瘦(削)的 (e.g. Her illness left her very thin. 她的病使她消瘦多了。)

6. sew：*Verb* make (a garment) by sewing 缝制 (e.g. My mother sewed a new cotton-padded jacket for me. 妈妈给我缝制一件新棉袄。)

■ 098 ::

从军词五首(其二) □令狐楚

孤心眠夜雪,满眼是秋沙。
万里犹防塞,三年不见家。

五绝原诗注释（Annotations to the Original Chinese Version）

令狐楚(约766—837)所作《从军词》共计五首,诗体为"孤心眠夜雪,满眼是秋沙。万里犹防塞,三年不见家"的这一首,是其中的第二首,描写的是长时间戍守边塞将士的思家之情以及当时边塞的状况。在诗人令狐楚生活的唐代那个时期,由于"连年战乱,人口锐减,无法征集更多新兵,使现役超期留用成为常事。"(文东,2015:153)这种情况在首联就初见端倪,"孤心"指孤自一个人,不见一同戍边之人,可见戍边将士后继无人的状况。到了尾联更是如此。尽管"万里"和"三年"皆有虚指的意味,但起码说明在很远的距离之内仍然是边防的要塞所在,没有人烟,而且戍边的将士已经有很长时间没有回家了。

Lines about Military Service on the Frontier(Second of Five Poems with the Same Title)

○By *LINGHU Chu*

Alone, I lie on th' snowy night,
Autumnal wind and sand in sight.
For thousands of miles far away,
It's still frontier, which I daresay,
And year in, year out, I'm still here
Without seeing my kinsfolk dear.

Annotations to Its Version of English Verse(韵体译诗注释)

1. line: *Noun* a part of a poem forming one horizontal row of written or printed words 诗行(e.g. Each stanza has eight lines. 每一诗节有八行。)

2. frontier: *Noun* a line or border separating two countries 边境;边界

3. th' = the

4. autumnal: *Adjective* of, characteristic of, or occurring in autumn 秋季的;秋季出现(或发生)的(e.g. rich autumnal colours 绚丽多彩的秋色)

5. daresay: *Verb* (used in the first person singular present tense) to think very likely or almost certain; suppose 猜想;料想

6. year in, year out: continuously or repeatedly over a period of years 年复一年;一年又一年(e.g. They rented the same bungalow year in, year out. 他们年年租用同一间平房。)

7. kinsfolk: *Noun* (in anthropological or formal use) a person's blood relations, regarded collectively(人类学用法或正式用法)家人;亲属

099 ::

从军行 □王昌龄
大将军出战,白日暗榆关。
三面黄金甲,单于破胆还。

五绝原诗注释(Annotations to the Original Chinese Version)

此诗为盛唐著名诗人王昌龄(约 690~698—756)所作五绝《从军行》①。诗题中,"从军行"属乐府相和歌辞中的平调曲,"多写军旅辛苦之情景。"(霍松林,1991:320)首联中,大将军率军出战,越过边关,白日变得暗淡起来。这也许是军中人数众多,扬尘所致,也许预示着一场恶战即将开始。次句中,据诗意"榆关"并非指今日的山海关等地,而是泛指北方边塞或边关。尾联中,诗人笔锋急转,遇敌开战,三面围攻,打得单于(参见本章第 095 首的注释)吓破了胆,落荒而逃。其中,"黄金甲"原指身披金甲的骑兵,用以指代战士。

Song of Frontier Warfare

○By *WANG Chang-ling*

Great General heads his men to
Attack their foemen, and th' daytime sky
Grows dim and dark when they go through
Th' frontier, soon finding foes nearby.
At once he starts a three-side raid,
And his gold-armoured men charge at
The foes, making them so afraid
That all their armed defense falls flat,
And that Chanyu is scared to death,
Fleeing from peril out of breath.

---

① 一作《从军行二首(其一)》,《全唐诗》第 143 卷录其诗题为《从军行》,且仅此一首,本书从之。

N. B. Chanyu is the title for the monarch of Hun Nationality, a member of a warlike Asiatic nomadic people who invaded and ravaged Europe in the 4th - 5th centuries, and had been invading ancient China for thousands of years. Here in this poem, Chanyu refers to the head of the nomadic troops, whom the Great General and his men attacked.

Annotations to Its Version of English Verse（韵体译诗注释）

1. frontier：*Noun* a line or border separating two countries 边境；边界

2. warfare：*Noun* [mass noun] engagement in or the activities involved in war or conflict 战争；作战；斗争

3. head：*Verb* (with obj.) be in the leading position on 率领；领导 (e.g. The St George's Day procession was headed by the mayor. 圣乔治日游行由市长带领。)

4. foeman：*Noun* (archaic or poetic) an enemy in war；foe (古旧用法或诗歌用法) 敌兵；敌人

5. th' = the

6. foe：*Noun* (poetic/literary or formal) an enemy or opponent (诗/文用法或正式用法) 敌人；对手 (e.g. Join forces against the common foe. 联合起来对付共同敌人。)

7. charge：*Verb* (no obj.) rush forward in attack 冲锋 (e.g. The plan is to charge headlong at the enemy. 计划是向敌人猛烈冲锋。)

8. fall flat：fail completely to produce the intended or expected effect 完全失败；完全未达到预期效果 (e.g. His jokes fell flat. 他的笑话都没有达到预期效果。)

9. peril：*Noun* (mass noun) serious and immediate danger (严重且迫在眉睫的) 危险；威胁 (e.g. You could well place us both in peril. 你很可能会使我们俩都处于危险之中。)

10. monarch：*Noun* a sovereign head of state, especially a king, queen, or emperor 君主；国王；皇帝；女王；女皇

11. nomadic：*Adjective* relating to or characteristic of nomads 游牧的；流浪的

■ 100 ::

哥舒歌 □西鄙人

北斗七星高，哥舒夜带刀。

至今窥牧马，不敢过临洮。

五绝原诗注释（Annotations to the Original Chinese Version）

泛泛而论，"西鄙人"是指唐朝西北边地之人，但《哥舒歌》一诗下所署"西鄙人"则确有其人，同样来自唐朝西北边地（"鄙"应为"边远的地方"之意），只不过其姓名、生平等均不详。据传此人开元天宝年间（公元742—756年）在世，著有《哥舒歌》广为传颂。西鄙人的这首五绝《哥舒歌》颇具雄浑、豪迈之气概。诗题中，"哥舒"据说指的是哥舒翰，是突厥族哥舒部人，"唐玄宗时大将，曾任陇右节度使兼河西节度使。"（霍松林，1991：352）首联以北斗七星之高衬托哥舒夜间带刀巡视边防之威风凛凛气势，尾联则言哥舒的威力所在：曾经的入侵者，到了现在只能远距离窥视这里的人民在牧马中悠闲地生活，再也不敢跨过边界、踏入临洮半步了。临洮（今甘肃岷县）的建制最早可追溯到秦王政八年（公元前239年），时称"临洮"，是秦朝修筑的长城西部的起点，唐朝时属陇右道，地理位置十分重要。

Song of General Geshu

○By *The Man from Northwestern Border of Tang Dynasty*

With th' Plough high up in th' sky of night,

By holding in hand his knife tight,

Geshu, for slight invaders' trace

Patrols the border with bold pace.

So, they dare not, until today,

Cross it to Lintao, but survey

Across it in a secret way

The horses that eat grass and neigh.

N. B. Geshu and Lintao: Geshu is a general at the most glorious stage of Tang Dynasty (618—907), and he is also appointed as the military head of Longyoudao, a wide range of area in Tang Dynasty including Lintao, which is mentioned in the poem. Furthermore, Lintao, today's Minxian County, Gansu Province, lies in the northwestern border of Tang Dynasty, and it is the starting point of the Great Wall of China in Qin Dynasty (221—207 B.C.).

Annotations to Its Version of English Verse（韵体译诗注释）

1. th' = the

2. plough：*Noun* (the Plough) a prominent formation of seven stars in the constellation Ursa Major (the Great Bear), containing the Pointers that indicate the direction to the Pole Star 北斗七星；北斗星

3. trace：*Noun* a mark, object, or other indication of the existence or passing of something 痕迹；踪迹 (e.g. Remove all traces of the old adhesive. 除去所有旧的粘合剂留下的痕迹。)

4. patrol：*Verb* (patrolled, patrolling) [with obj.] keep watch over (an area) by regularly walking or travelling around it 在……巡逻；巡查 (e.g. The garrison had to patrol the streets to maintain order. 卫戍部队不得不巡查街道来维持秩序。)

5. pace：*Noun* (mass noun) (poetic/literary) a person's manner of walking or running（诗/文用法）步态 (e.g. I steal with quiet pace. 我悄悄地走。)

6. survey：*Verb* [with obj.] (of a person or their eyes) look carefully and thoroughly at (someone or something), especially so as to appraise them 审视 (e.g. Her green eyes surveyed him coolly. 她一双绿色的眼睛冷静地打量着他。)

7. neigh：*Verb* (no obj.) (of a horse) make a characteristic high whinnying sound；utter a neigh（马）嘶；嘶鸣

101 ::

马诗二十三首（其五）　　□李贺

大漠沙如雪，燕山月似钩。
何当金络脑，快走踏清秋。

五绝原诗注释（Annotations to the Original Chinese Version）

有"诗鬼"之称的唐代诗人李贺（约791—约817）在《马诗二十三首》中，借"马"抒情，表达了自己的人生感慨以及愤懑之情。这一主题的诗共有二十三首，诗体为"大漠沙如雪，燕山月似钩。何当金络脑，快走踏清秋"的这一首，是其中的第五首。此诗首联写景，同时交代了诗人欲得以施展抱负的地点，尾联则借马之口，抒发了自己内心的想法和抱负。

首联两句像某些古诗词里的用法一样,应做互文见义来处理,即"大漠"和"燕山"皆"沙如雪""月似钩"(钩,在此为古代的一种兵器,刀刃呈弧形弯曲,形似月牙,以吴钩为典范)。其中,大漠,班固《封燕然山铭》:"经卤碛,绝大漠。"①(本书著者注:"卤碛"似乎应为"碛卤")李善注:"大漠,沙漠也。"②沙如雪,梁元帝《玄览赋》:"看白沙而似雪。"③尾联中,"何当"意为何时可以戴上或能够得到,"金络脑"即金络头、金辔头,也就是金质的或饰金的马笼头之类,属贵重马具之列,言马受重用,意指人得到赏识而施展抱负,最终得以"快走踏清秋"(一作"快走踏青秋")。另外,从"大漠"这一意象来考量,将"燕山"一词理解成"燕然山"(今蒙古人民共和国境内西部的杭爱山)比"燕山"(位于今河北省及北京市)更为合理一些,而且大漠、燕(然)山也是孕育、出产宝马良驹的地方。

Poetry of Inward Thoughts of a Horse(Fifth of Twenty-three Poems with the Same Title)

○By *LI He*

In th' vast of desert in th' far north

And Yanshan Mountain, sand grains seem

Fine snow, while th' crescent moon comes forth,

Which looks like sickle-shaped arms to gleam.

When can a charger with th' will wear

A golden bridle, running there,

Th' vast of north border, to display

His glory in fight with a neigh

On such a chilly autumn day?

N. B. Yanshan Mountain: In this poem, it may refer to the mountain in the northern part of Beijing, which is in the north of China, or it

---

① 转引自"霍松林,1991:787"。
② 转引自"霍松林,1991:787"。
③ 转引自"霍松林,1991:787"。

may be the Yanranshan Mountain for short, a mountain in the northern (or northwestern to be more accurate) border of ancient China (Today's Hang'ai Mountain in the west of the People's Republic of Mongolia), where there is a vast area of desert and top army horses are bred.

Annotations to Its Version of English Verse（韵体译诗注释）

1. inward：*Adjective* existing within the mind, soul, or spirit, and often not expressed 内心的;精神的;灵魂中的（e.g. She felt an inward sense of release. 她内心感到一种解脱。）

2. th' = the

3. vast：*Noun* (usu. the/a vast)（chiefly poetic) immense or boundless space（主要为诗歌用法)茫茫;无边无际的空间

4. fine：*Adjective* consisting of small particles 由微小颗粒构成的（e.g. The soils were all fine silt. 土壤全是颗粒微小的泥沙。）

5. crescent：*Noun* the curved sickle shape of the waxing or waning moon 月牙形;新月形;弦月形;(月亮)镰刀形

6. forth：*Adverb* (chiefly archaic) out from a starting point and forwards or into view（主要为古旧用法)向外;向前;向前方;露出（The sun came forth from behind the cloud. 太阳从云后露出来。）

7. sickle：*Noun* a short-handled farming tool with a semicircular blade, used for cutting corn, lopping, or trimming 镰刀

8. arms：*Plural Noun* weapons; armaments 武器;军械

9. gleam：*Verb* [no obj.] shine brightly, especially with reflected light（尤指反光的)发光;闪烁

10. charger：*Noun* a horse ridden by a knight or cavalryman 骑士坐骑;骑兵战马

11. will：*Noun* (also willpower) [mass noun] control deliberately exerted to do something or to restrain one's own impulses 意志力;毅力;自制力（e.g. a stupendous effort of will 惊人的毅力）

12. bridle：*Noun* the headgear used to control a horse, consisting of buckled straps to which a bit and reins are attached 马勒;马笼头;辔头

13. neigh：*Noun* a characteristic high whinnying sound made by a horse 马嘶声

14. chilly：*Adjective* (chillier, chilliest) uncomfortably or unpleasantly cold 寒冷的

参考文献

[01] BRESLIN R. Translation[M]. New York: Garden Press, 1976.
[02] BYNNER W. The Jade Mountain: A Chinese Anthology[M]. New York: Alfred A. Knopf, 1929.
[03] CHANG H C. Nature Poetry—Chinese Literature [M] Vol. 2. Edinburgh: Edinburgh University Press, 1977.
[04] CHIH F. Tu Fu: Selected Poems[M]. Honolulu, Hawaii: University Press of the Pacific, 2004.
[05] GILES H A. Chinese Poetry in English Verse (1898) [M]. Whitefish Montana: Kessinger Publishing, 2009.
[06] GRAHAM A C. Poems of the Late T'ang[M]. New York: NYRB Classics, 2008.
[07] HARRIS P. Three Hundred Tang Poems (Everyman's Library Pocket Poets) [M]. New York: Random House, 2009.
[08] HINTON D. The Selected Poems of Li Po[M]. New York: New Directions Publishing Corporation, 1996.
[09] HINTON D. Classical Chinese Poetry: An Anthology[M]. New York: Farrar, Straus and Giroux, 2010.
[10] JENYNS S. A Further Selection from the Three Hundred Poems

of the T'ang Dynasty[M]. London: John Murray, 1944.

[11] JOHNSON S M. Fifty Tang Poems[M]. San Francisco: Pocketscholar Press, 2000.

[12] LARSEN J. Willow, Wine, Mirror, Moon: Women's Poems from Tang China (Lannan Translations Selection Series) [M]. Rochester: BOA Editions Ltd., 2005.

[13] LARSEN J. Brocade River Poems: Selected Works of the Tang Dynasty Courtesan (Lockert Library of Poetry in Translation) [M]. Princeton: Princeton University Press, 1987.

[14] LEGGE J. The Chinese Classics, Tr. Into English, with Preliminary Essays and Explanatory Notes by James Legge[M]. Ann Arbor, Michigan: University of Michigan Library, 2006.

[15] LOWELL A, AYSCOUGH F W. Fir-Flower Tablets: Poems Translated from the Chinese [M]. Carolina, Charleston, SC: Nabu Press, 2010.

[16] NEWMARK P. A Textbook of Translation[M]. London: Prentice Hall, 1988.

[17] NIDA E A, TABER C R. The Theory and Practice of Translation [M]. Leiden: Brill Academic Pub, 2003.

[18] OBATA S. The Works of Li Po: The Chinese Poet[M]. Carolina, Charleston, SC: Nabu Press, 2010.

[19] OWEN S. The Great Age of Chinese Poetry: The High T'ang [M]. New Haven and London: Yale University Press, 1981.

[20] OWEN S. An Anthology of Chinese Literature: Beginnings To 1911[M]. New York and London: W. W. Norton & Company, 1996.

[21] POUND E. Cathay (1915) [M]. Whitefish, Montana: Kessinger Publishing, 2010.

[22] REXROTH K. 100 Poems from the Chinese[M]. New York: New Directions Publishing Corporation, 1971.

[23] VENUTI L et al. Rethinking Translation: Discourse, Subjectivity and Ideology[M]. London and New York: Routledge, 1992.

[24] WALEY A. A Hundred and Seventy Chinese Poems[M]. Whitefish, Montana: Kessinger Publishing, 2007.

[25] WATSON B. Cold Mountain: 100 Poems by the T'ang Poet Hanshan[M]. New York: Columbia University Press, 1970.

[26] WYLIE A. Notes on Chinese Literature: With Introductory Remarks[M]. Charleston: BiblioLife, 2009.

[27] YIP W-L. Chinese Poetry: An Anthology of Major Modes and Genres (2nd Revised Edition) [M]. Durham: Duke University Press, 1997.

[28] YU P. The Poetry of Wang Wei: New Translations and Commentary[M]. Bloomington: Indiana University Press, 1980.

[29] 阿忆. 风雨北大 水木清华[M]. 贵阳：贵州教育出版社, 2012.

[30] 艾克利, 段宪文, 王友怀. 唐诗三百首注译[M]. 北京：太白文艺出版社, 2005.

[31] 白建忠. 何谓"石尤风"？[J]. 古典文学知识, 2013(4)：151-156.

[32] 白靖宇. 文化与翻译[M]. 北京：中国社会科学出版社, 2000.

[33] 包惠南, 包昂. 实用文化翻译学[M]. 上海：上海科学普及出版社, 2000.

[34] 蔡廷干(Tsai Ting-Kan). 唐诗英韵(Chinese Poems in English Rhyme)[M]. 芝加哥(Chicago)：芝加哥大学出版社(University of Chicago Press), 1932.

[35] 曹顺发. 走近"形美"：古汉诗英译实践点滴[M]. 北京：国防工业出版社, 2007.

[36] 陈安定. 英汉修辞与翻译[M]. 北京：中国青年出版社, 2004.

[37] 陈邦炎. 唐人绝句鉴赏集[M]. 太原：北岳文艺出版社, 1988.

[38] 陈婉俊. 唐诗三百首[M]. 北京：中华书局, 1959.

[39] 陈望道. 修辞学发凡[M]. 上海：上海教育出版社，1997.

[40] 陈伟英. 唐诗主语省略英译补出现象——解读文化差异及意境不可译性[J]. 浙江大学学报（人文社会科学版），2006(6)：177—186.

[41] 初大告. 中华隽词101[M]. 北京：新世界出版社，1987.

[42] 丛滋杭. 中国古典诗歌英译理论研究[M]. 北京：国防工业出版社，2007.

[43] 单畅，王永胜. 唐代五绝品读及英译探索（上）[M]. 长春：吉林大学出版社，2013.

[44] 单畅，王永胜. 英文电影片名汉译的审美取向[J]. 当代电影，2013(6)：126-129.

[45] 单畅，王永胜. 英文短篇哲理诗101首汉译并注（英汉双语）[M]. 北京：中国商业出版社，2015.

[46] 邓安生，刘畅，杨永明. 王维诗选译[M]. 成都：巴蜀书社，1990.

[47] 邓炎昌，刘润清. 语言与文化——英汉语言文化对比[M]. 北京：外语教学与研究出版社，1989.

[48] 都森，陈玉筠. 古韵新声——唐诗绝句英译108首（英汉对照）[M]. 武汉：华中科技大学出版社，2011.

[49] 樊养才.《春怨》一诗八种英译评析[J]. 西安外国语学院学报，2000(3)：6-9.

[50] 范文澜. 中国通史（第四册）[M]. 北京：人民出版社，2004.

[51] 范之麟. 李益诗注[M]. 上海：上海古籍出版社，1984.

[52] 范祖民. 实用英语修辞[M]. 北京：科学出版社，2010.

[53] 冯翠华. 英语修辞大全[M]. 北京：外语教学与研究出版社，2004.

[54] 冯庆华. 文体翻译论[M]. 上海：上海外语教育出版社，2002.

[55] 冯庆华. 实用翻译教程[M]. 上海：上海外语教育出版社，2008.

[56] 福建师范大学中文系古典文学教研室. 中国古代文学作品选析(中册)[M]. 福州：福建教育出版社, 1986.
[57] 付朝. 孙子兵法结构研究[M]. 北京：解放军出版社, 2010.
[58] 傅璇琮. 唐代诗人丛考[M]. 北京：中华书局, 1996.
[59] 高玉昆. 论唐诗英译[J]. 国际安全研究, 1994(4)：21-29.
[60] 葛杰, 仓阳卿. 中国古典文学作品选读：绝句三百首[M]. 上海：上海古籍出版社, 1980.
[61] 葛景春. 李白诗选[M]. 北京：中华书局, 2005.
[62] 葛晓音. 诗国高潮与盛唐文化[M]. 北京：北京大学出版社, 1998.
[63] 龚景浩. 英译唐诗名作选[M]. 北京：商务印书馆, 2006.
[64] 顾建国. 张九龄研究[M]. 北京：中华书局, 2007.
[65] 顾青. 唐诗三百首[M]. 北京：中华书局, 2009.
[66] 顾正阳. 古诗词曲英译美学研究[M]. 上海：上海大学出版社, 2006.
[67] 顾正阳. 古诗词曲英译文化探索[M]. 上海：上海大学出版社, 2007.
[68] 郭莉. 浅谈唐代巴蜀才子——记《唐才子传》中的巴蜀才子[J]. 天府新论, 2006(S2)：190—192.
[69] 郭著章, 江安, 鲁文忠. 唐诗精品百首英译(修订版)[M]. 武汉：武汉大学出版社, 2010.
[70] 韩成武, 张国伟. 唐诗三百首赏析[M]. 石家庄：河北人民出版社, 1995.
[71] 韩泉欣. 孟郊集校注[M]. 杭州：浙江古籍出版社, 1995.
[72] 何功杰. 英语诗歌导读[M]. 苏州：苏州大学出版社, 2011.
[73] 侯真平. 梦溪笔谈[M]. 长沙：岳麓书社, 2002.
[74] 胡小礼. 英文数字习语的结构类型及其译法初探[J]. 中国科技信息, 2008(22)：236-237.
[75] 胡筱颖. 国内唐诗英译研究回顾与反思(1980—2011)[J]. 译苑新谭, 2013(5)：087—094.

[76] 黄杲炘. 英诗汉译学[M]. 上海：上海外语教育出版社, 2007.

[77] 黄国文. 翻译研究的语言学探索——古诗英译本的语言学分析[M]. 上海：上海外语教育出版社, 2006.

[78] 黄国文. 功能语言学分析对翻译研究的启示——《清明》英译文的经验功能分析[J]. 外语与外语教学, 2002(5)：1-6, 11.

[79] 黄国文. 唐诗英译文中的引述现象分析[J]. 外语学刊, 2002(3)：1-7.

[80] 黄皓峰. 刘方平研究[J]. 古籍研究, 2005(2)：69-80.

[81] 黄鸣奋. 英语世界唐诗专题译、论著通考[J]. 国外社会科学, 1995(1)：58-62.

[82] 霍松林. 万首唐人绝句校注集评(上册)[M]. 太原：山西人民出版社, 1991.

[83] [宋]计有功. 唐诗纪事[M]. 上海：上海古籍出版社, 1987.

[84] 江湖夜雨. 千年霜月千家诗：七言千家诗的全新解读[M]. 天津：天津教育出版社, 2010.

[85] 江岚, 罗时进. 早期英国汉学家对唐诗英译的贡献[J]. 上海大学学报(社会科学版), 2009(02)：33-42.

[86] 金琳. 古诗词中叠音词的审美特性分析[J]. 语文知识, 2003(10)：8-9.

[87] 金性尧. 唐诗三百首新注[M]. 上海：上海古籍出版社, 1993.

[88] 施建中, 隋淑芬. 金圣叹选批唐诗六百首[M]. 北京：北京出版社, 1989.

[89] 景晓莺, 王丹斌. 英语诗歌常识与名作研读[M]. 上海：上海交通大学出版社, 2011.

[90] 雷磊. 论玉台体[J]. 求索, 2004(3)：183-185, 170.

[91] 李建军. 《诗经》与周代原始宗教文化的演化[J]. 江西师范大学学报(哲学社会科学版), 2005(2)：17-22.

[92] 李建军. 文化翻译论[M]. 上海：复旦大学出版社，2010.
[93] 李景白. 孟浩然诗集校注[M]. 成都：巴蜀书社，1988.
[94] 李梦生. 绝句三百首注评[M]. 南京：凤凰出版社，2007.
[95] 李淼. 唐诗三百首[M]. 长春：吉林文史出版社，2007.
[96] 李贻荫. "珠帘"与"蛾眉"的英译[J]. 翻译通讯，1984(12)：25-25.
[97] 李裕民. 王之涣作《登鹳雀楼》？——千古名诗原作者考辨[J]. 史志学刊，2015(1)：67-73.
[98] 李云逸. 卢照邻集校注[M]. 北京：中华书局，1998.
[99] 李云逸. 王昌龄诗注[M]. 上海：上海古籍出版社，1984.
[100] 梁守涛. 英诗格律浅说[M]. 北京：商务印书馆，1979.
[101] 廖梦麟. 唐诗《清明》三个英译本的语篇功能分析[J]. 琼州学院学报，2013(3)：64-67.
[102] 林巍. 中西文化比较及翻译研究[M]. 上海：华东理工大学出版社，2009.
[103] 刘军平. 新译唐诗英韵百首[M]. 北京：中华书局，2002.
[104] 刘开扬. 高适诗集编年笺注[M]. 北京：中华书局，1981.
[105] 刘明华. 丛生的文体：唐宋五大文体的繁荣[M]. 南京：江苏教育出版社，2000.
[106] 刘首顺. 唐诗三百首全译[M]. 西安：陕西人民教育出版社，1986.
[107] [清]刘熙载. 艺概[M]. 上海：上海古籍出版社，1978.
[108] 刘永济. 唐人绝句精华[M]. 北京：人民文学出版社，1981.
[109] 卢炳群. 英译李贺诗百首[M]. 北京：国防工业出版社，2013.
[110] 卢军羽，席欢明. 汉语古诗词英译理论的构建：述评与展望[J]. 广东外语外贸大学学报，2008(2)：75-78.
[111] 罗韬. 张九龄诗文选[M]. 广州：广东人民出版社，1994.
[112] 罗宗强. 语言文学丛著·唐诗小史[M]. 西安：陕西人民出版社，1987.

[113] 吕晴飞,李观鼎,刘方成.汉魏六朝诗歌鉴赏辞典[M].北京:中国和平出版社,1990.

[114] 吕叔湘.中诗英译比录[M].北京:中华书局,2002.

[115] 毛谷风.略论唐人五言绝句[J].浙江师范大学学报(社会科学版),1989(1):8-12.

[116] 毛华奋.汉语古诗英译比读与研究[M].上海:上海社会科学院出版社,2007.

[117] 茅于美.人文大讲堂·中西诗歌比较研究(第二版)[M].北京:中国人民大学出版社,2012.

[118] 蒙万夫,阎琦.千家诗鉴赏辞典[M].西安:陕西人民教育出版社,1991.

[119] 摩西.唐诗的江山[M].北京:中国对外翻译出版公司,2008.

[120] 穆克宏.盛唐著名诗人王昌龄[J].福建师大学报(哲学社会科学版),1981(4):85—93,84.

[121] 人民文学出版社编辑部.唐诗名译[M].北京:人民文学出版社,2000.

[122] 任国绪.卢照邻集编年笺注[M].哈尔滨:黑龙江人民出版社,1989.

[123] 任国绪.初唐四杰诗选[M].西安:陕西人民出版社,1992.

[124] 沙灵娜.唐诗三百首全译[M].贵阳:贵州人民出版社,1983.

[125] 商务印书馆辞书研究中心.新华成语词典[M].北京:商务印书馆,2002.

[126] 尚作恩,李孝堂,吴绍礼.晚唐诗译释[M].哈尔滨:黑龙江人民出版社,1987.

[127] [清]沈德潜.唐诗别裁集(全二册)[M].上海:上海古籍出版社,1979.

[128] 沈阳市作家协会.时光行板:盛京文学网.2016卷[M].长春:吉林人民出版社,2018.

[129] 施议对. 人间词话译注(增订本)[M]. 长沙：岳麓书社, 2008.

[130] 施蛰存. 唐诗百话[M]. 上海：上海古籍出版社, 1987.

[131] 孙大雨. 古诗文英译集[M]. 上海：上海外语教育出版社, 2000.

[132] 孙钦善. 高适集校注[M]. 上海：上海古籍出版社, 1984.

[133] 孙艺风. 视角 阐释 文化：文学翻译与翻译理论[M]. 北京：清华大学出版社, 2004.

[134] 谭燕保. "断裂"与"异化"：唐诗的"救赎"[J]. 武汉理工大学学报(社会科学版), 2013(3)：481—486.

[135] 《唐诗鉴赏大全集》编委会. 唐诗鉴赏大全集[M]. 北京：中国华侨出版社, 2010.

[136] 唐一鹤. 英译唐诗三百首[M]. 天津：天津人民出版社, 2005.

[137] 陶敏, 王友胜. 韦应物诗选[M]. 北京：中华书局, 2005.

[138] 田耕宇. 唐音余韵：晚唐诗研究[M]. 成都：巴蜀书社, 2001.

[139] 汪敬钦. 《春怨》英译启示录——理解之于译诗[J]. 外语教学, 2000(01)：60-63.

[140] 汪榕培, 李正栓. 典籍英译研究[M]. 保定：河北大学出版社, 2005.

[141] 王宝童. 王维诗百首(汉英对照图文本)[M]. 上海：上海世界图书出版公司, 2005.

[142] 王臣. 月锦绣, 锁清秋[M]. 武汉：武汉出版社, 2011.

[143] 王臣. 染花集：最好的女子, 最美的情事[M]. 北京：中国华侨出版社, 2011.

[144] 王大濂. 英译唐诗绝句百首[M]. 天津：百花文艺出版社, 1998.

[145] 王定璋. 略论李端和他的诗歌[J]. 青海民族学院学报, 1989(1)：43-49.

[146] 王海艳,刘秀华.仁者见仁 智者见智——浅析中诗英译现状[J].辽宁工业大学学报(社会科学版),2009(3):48—50.

[147] 王洪,田军.唐诗百科大辞典[M].北京:光明日报出版社,1990.

[148] 王建平.汉诗英译中的语篇衔接与连贯[J].外国语言文学,2003(1):36-40.

[149] 王力,岑麒祥,林焘.古汉语常用字字典[M].4版,北京:商务印书馆,2005.

[150] 王宁.翻译研究的文化转向[M].北京:清华大学出版社,2009.

[151] 王庆凯.诗词格式谱典[M].广州:花城出版社,2008.

[152] 王守义,约翰·诺弗尔.唐宋诗词英译[M].哈尔滨:黑龙江人民出版社,1989.

[153] 王文斌.从两首唐诗的不同英译看文学翻译中的未定性和具体化[J].中国翻译,2001(2):52-54.

[154] 王小可.早期英国唐诗英译中的阴性化倾向[J].衡水学院学报,2013(5):83-86.

[155] 王小如,王运熙,骆玉明,等.汉魏六朝诗鉴赏辞典[M].上海:上海辞书出版社,1992.

[156] 王永胜,赵朋亮.英文电影作品片名翻译比较研究[J].渤海大学学报(哲学社会科学版),2007(6):141-144.

[157] 王永义.格律诗写作技巧[M].青岛:青岛出版社,1995.

[158] 文东.当你读懂唐诗千首:古绝与律绝[M].广州:羊城晚报出版社,2015.

[159] 文殊.唐宋绝句名篇英译[M].北京:外语教学与研究出版社,1995.

[160] 文殊.诗词英译选[M].北京:外语教学与研究出版社,1989.

[161] 翁显良.古诗英译[M].北京:北京出版社,1985.

[162] 翁显良.古诗英译二十八首[J].外国语(上海外国语学院学报),1988(6):11-15,10.
[163] 吴伏生.汉诗英译研究:理雅各、翟理斯、韦利、庞德[M].北京:学苑出版社,2012.
[164] 吴钧陶.汉英对照·唐诗三百首[M].长沙:湖南出版社,1997.
[165] 萧涤非,俞平伯,施蛰存,等.唐诗鉴赏辞典[M].上海:上海辞书出版社,2004.
[166] 熊飞.张九龄集校注[M].北京:中华书局,2008.
[167] 徐昌才.恋上大唐诗生活[M].西安:陕西师范大学出版总社有限公司,2011.
[168] 徐定祥.论李峤及其诗歌[J].江淮论坛,1992(6):95—102.
[169] 徐磊.只是当时已惘然:唐诗的美丽读法[M].北京:中国对外翻译出版公司,2007.
[170] 徐明霞.卢照邻集 杨炯集[M].北京:中华书局,1980.
[171] 徐鹏.孟浩然集校注[M].北京:人民文学出版社,1989.
[172] 徐四海.毛泽东诗词鉴赏[M].昆明:云南人民出版社,2005.
[173] 徐忠杰.唐诗二百首英译[M].北京:北京语言学院出版社,1990.
[174] 许敏.国内认知视阈下的古诗英译研究综述[J].宜春学院学报,2014(01):115—118.
[175] 许渊冲.李白诗选[M].长沙:湖南人民出版社,2007.
[176] 许渊冲,陆佩弦,吴钧陶,等.唐诗三百首新译(英汉对照)[M].北京:中国对外翻译出版公司,1988.
[177] 许渊冲.典籍英译,中国可算世界一流[J].中国外语,2006(5):70-72.
[178] 许渊冲.中诗英韵探胜——从《诗经》到《西厢记》[M].北京:北京大学出版社,1992.

[179] 许渊冲. 唐诗三百首[M]. 北京:高等教育出版社,2000.
[180] 闫敬芳. 白居易闲适诗中的友情[J]. 文山学院学报,2010(1):69-71,109.
[181] 杨彩玉,陈琪. 从李白的诗歌看唐诗中数字的翻译[J]. 内蒙古农业大学学报(社会科学版),2004(4):117-119.
[182] 杨成虎. 中国诗歌典籍英译散论[M]. 北京:国防工业出版社,2012.
[183] 杨宪益,戴乃迭. 古诗苑汉英译丛:唐诗(中英文对照)[M]. 北京:外文出版社,2003.
[184] 杨秀梅,包通法. 中国古典诗歌英译研究历史与现状[J]. 外语与外语教学,2009(12):57-60.
[185] 易经. 诗歌翻译"三美"例释[J]. 常德师范学院学报(社会科学版),2002(3):57-59.
[186] 余浩然. 格律诗词写作[M]. 长沙:岳麓书社,2001.
[187] 俞陛云. 大家小书·诗境浅说[M]. 北京:北京出版社,2011.
[188] 喻守真. 唐诗三百首详析[M]. 北京:中华书局,1957.
[189] 袁楚林. 中唐诗人雍裕之生平及著述考[J]. 北京化工大学学报(社会科学版),2015(4):79-82.
[190] 袁行霈. 中国文学史(第1卷)[M]. 2版,北京:高等教育出版社,2005.
[191] 詹福瑞,刘崇德,葛景春,等. 李白诗全译[M]. 石家庄:河北人民出版社,1997.
[192] 张安祖. 唐诗中的红豆考原[J]. 文献,2007(1):186-189.
[193] 张保红. 点染法:翁显良汉诗英译艺术研究[J]. 中国外语,2014(4):87-94,111.
[194] 张富祥. 梦溪笔谈[M]. 北京:中华书局,2009.
[195] 张固也. 中晚唐诗人于武陵考[J]. 吉林大学社会科学学报,2008(5):91-98.
[196] 张光明. 英汉修辞思想比较与翻译[M]. 北京:军事谊文出

版社，2002.

[197] 张国浩. 李端诗人名考[J]. 信阳师范学院学报(哲学社会科学版)，2009(2)：115-118.

[198] 《中国翻译》编辑部. 诗词翻译的艺术[M]. 北京：中国对外翻译出版公司，1987.

[199] 张平. 浅析孟浩然《宿建德江》七个译本的叙述主体问题[J]. 文学前言，2008(2)：217-222.

[200] 张廷琛，魏博思. 唐诗一百首：汉英对照[M]. 北京：中国对外翻译出版公司，2007.

[201] 张永刚，杨克宇，郎少俊，等. 中国古代文学简史与作品选(上册)[M]. 呼和浩特：内蒙古大学出版社，2012.

[202] 张玉兰. 翻译美学理论对唐诗英译意境再现的指导作用[J]. 北京化工大学学报(社会科学版)，2013(2)：57-60，72.

[203] 张跃伟，王永胜. 罗尔德·达尔短篇故事品读及汉译探索(第8卷)[M]. 哈尔滨：哈尔滨工业大学出版社，2016.

[204] 张智中. 唐人白话绝句百首英译[M]. 北京：国防工业出版社，2009.

[205] 赵昌平. 李白诗选评[M]. 上海：上海古籍出版社，2002.

[206] 赵昌平. 唐诗三百首全解[M]. 上海：复旦大学出版社，2006.

[207] 赵建莉. 中国古典文学作品选析丛书·初唐诗歌赏析[M]. 南宁：广西教育出版社，1990.

[208] 赵晓茹. 浅议诗歌翻译中的直译和意译[J]. 北京城市学院学报，2010(4)：88-92.

[209] 赵亚丽，苏占兵. 婉约词赏读[M]. 北京：中国华侨出版社，2008.

[210] 赵燕，栗洪武. 《李峤百咏》的启蒙思想与诗学价值[J]. 江西社会科学，2013(10)：79-83.

[211] 周彦文，贺雄飞. 年轻的潇洒——与汪国真对白[M]. 北

京：国际文化出版公司，1991.

[212] 周志培. 汉英对比与翻译中的转换[M]. 华东理工大学出版社，2003.

[213] 朱徽. 中英诗艺比较研究[M]. 成都：四川大学出版社，2010.

[214] 朱徽. 唐诗在美国的翻译与接受[J]. 四川大学学报，2004(4)：84-89.

[215] 朱媛媛. 汉诗英译研究现状[J]. 语文学刊(外语教育教学)，2011(5)：79-80.

[216] 祝尚书. 卢照邻集笺注[M]. 上海：上海古籍出版社，1994.

[217] 卓振英. 汉诗英译论纲[M]. 杭州：浙江大学出版社，2011.

后　　记

　　一千二百多年前，唐代大诗人李白发出这样的感慨："噫吁嚱，危乎高哉！蜀道之难，难于上青天！"

　　一千二百多年以后的今天，我们从事翻译研究，面对翻译实践，联想到太白之感慨，颇感译事之难，不亚于蜀道之难。于是，借题发挥，不禁发出这样的感慨："噫吁嚱，艰乎难哉！译事之难，犹蜀道之难，难于上青天！"这样的感慨，其实一点儿都不为过。

　　有过之而无不及的，就是译事之中的译诗，乃难中之难，更是难于上青天了。同时，译诗也是文学翻译领域里的难点，可谓难上加难。

　　欲对唐代五绝进行英译研究，最终进行韵体英译探索，必先从浩如烟海的唐代五绝中筛选出一定数量的五绝诗作为样本，并加以简单的归类。这些样本诗不一定都十分出众，也不一定都名垂诗史，但都具有一定的代表性，有助于达到本书的目的。对这些具有代表性唐代五绝作品的英语译文，即英译诗，本书著者着力进行韵译方面的探索。在韵译的探索中，首先力求意义和意象方面的贴切，再考虑形式的因素，特别是英译诗格律方面的因素。

　　在筛选和翻译这些具有代表性的唐代五绝作品过程中，本书著者历尽了艰辛，特别是在韵体英译即韵译过程中，不时会遇到这样或那样的"坎坷"。诗人在创作过程中,为了格律的需要,避开了一些常用词,转而采用生僻的古词或古人熟谙的典故,这就硬逼着译者硬着头皮去琢磨这样的词或典故该如何处理。另外,在译诗过程中,还要观照原诗的形式,特别是韵律方面,同时还要兼顾译语(即英语)诗歌的形式,特别是译语读者的诗歌审美习惯。对于这样的"坎坷",下笔前译者会来回踱步、反复思量、仔细斟酌。正如鲁迅先生在译完《死魂灵》谈到翻译时所言:"我向来总以为翻译比创作容易,因为至少是无须构想。但到真的一译,就会遇着难关,譬如一个名词或动词,写不出,创作时候可以回避,翻译上却不成,也还得想,一直弄到头昏眼花,好像在脑子里面摸一个急于要开箱子的钥匙,却没有。"(鲁迅《"题未定"草·且介亭杂文二集》)

在筛选和翻译这些具有代表性的唐代五绝作品过程中,还会遇到语言及文化差异方面的"绊脚石",特别是具有典型汉文化因素的典故,处理起来颇费脑筋。正如严复在谈《天演论》翻译的《译例言》中所言:"新理踵出,名目纷繁,索之中文,渺不可得,即有牵合,终嫌参差,译者遇此,独有自具衡量,即义定名。"当然,与严复先生"索之中文"不同的是,本书著者在此是"索之英文"。另外,在翻译中对于查询无果的地方,也得认真加以思考,甚至经过了很长时间才"创造性"地下笔定论,可谓"一名之立,旬月踟蹰。我罪我知,是存明哲。"(严复《译例言》)。由此可见,译事之难也好,或译诗之难也罢,都不亚于李太白笔下的"蜀道之难,难于上青天"了!

幸运的是,在筛选和翻译这些具有代表性的唐代五绝作品过程中,我们得到了许多朋友和同事热情的帮助和有力的支持,感激之情无以言表。特别感谢本书课题组全体成员!同时,我们十分感谢渤海大学外国语学院领导和同事给予我们热情的帮助和有力的支持!十分感谢陕西学前师范学院教育科学学院领导和同事给予我们热情的帮助和有力的支持!十分感谢为本书的出版而忙碌的所有编辑人员和工作人员!最后,十分感谢为本书提供帮助的所有朋友和同仁!

当然,由于时间和能力所限,错误在所难免,还望读者赐教、斧正,并多提宝贵意见。本书肯定存在这样或那样的不足,但是,我们本着扎实做学问、做学问如做人的思想,从起点出发,力求稳扎稳打,力戒浮躁之风,勿求好高骛远。

记得《礼记·中庸》里有言:"君子之道,譬如行远,必自迩,譬如登高,必自卑。"愿以此语共勉。

著者

王永胜　李艳

2019 年岁初